A Workbook of New Testament Greek
for self-study, with complete keys

Level 1

E. J. Pond

TABLE OF CONTENTS

LIST OF TABLES

LIST OF SOUND FILES
Available on the website:
http://koineworkbook.wordpress.com/

ABBREVIATIONS and SYMBOLS

acc.   accusative
dat.   dative
fem.   feminine
gen.   genitive
masc.   masculine
neut.   neuter
nom.   nominative
pl.   plural
sing.   singular

[ ]   Brackets enclose either (1) a word in English, where the corresponding
            word is present in Greek but is generally omitted in the English
            translation or (2) a word in English, where the corresponding word is
            not present in Greek but generally added in the English translation.

            I usually exempt the added English indefinite article ('a', 'an') from this
            practice. I also exempt the understood pronoun subjects of a verb.

ἀρχὴ ἥμισυ παντός

ΤΟΔΕΕΤΙΑΠΑΙΔΗΝ·
ΤΗΝΤΩΝΣΑΛΕΥ
ΟΜΕΝΩΝΜΕΤΑΟ·
ΣΙΝΩΣΠΕΠΟΙΗ
ΜΕΝΩΝΙΝΑΜΙΝΗ
ΤΑΜΗΣΑΛΕΥΟΜΕΝΑ
ΔΙΟΒΑΣΙΛΕΙΑΝΑΣΑ
ΛΕΥΤΟΝΠΑΡΑΛΑ
ΒΑΝΟΝΤΕΣΕΧΟΜΕ
ΧΑΡΙΝΔΙΗΣΛΑΤΡΕΥ
ΟΜΕΝΕΥΑΡΕΣΤΩ·

Fig. 1. A few lines (Hebrews 12: 27-28) from the Codex Sinaiticus, written in *koine* Greek. This is an uncial manuscript (using all capital letters), without spaces between words, as was standard practice at the time (4th century AD).

INTRODUCTION

Welcome to Greek. Welcome to a language with a history of over three thousand years; the language of Homer, Plato, Aristotle--and so many others!--in addition to being the language of the New Testament. And welcome to *koine* Greek--the 'common' Greek dialect of a few hundred years before and after the birth of Christ.

This series of workbooks focuses on exercises and practice for the self-study learner, and for individuals who wish to review coursework, or prepare for coursework to be taken in New Testament Greek. **We start from the beginning, with no previous knowledge of Greek assumed.** The book can be used as a stand-alone source for learning the language, or be supplemented with other texts. The present volume is the first of a series.

What the workbook is intended to do:

1) To present a basic grammar, and a reading program, for the Greek language as used in the New Testament.

2) To present this grammar in a workbook form and, following the introductory sections, to include exercises on most pages.

3) To provide immediate feedback to the reader doing the exercises, in the form of a key found on the same or next page.

4) When possible, to use examples from the New Testament itself in the exercises, but to be flexible on this point early on. Translations in the first 10 lessons (or so) will be primarily of isolated words and short phrases.

5) To pay particular attention to the middle stages of language learning. It is my experience that language textbooks tend to go slowly and carefully over the first few topics; then--seemingly--pass without warning into advanced work. This series will provide extended exercises at the intermediate levels.

6) To provide information and resources for further study.

What the present book is <u>not</u> intended to do:

1) To be in itself a systematic or complete grammar of koine Greek, or to include all details, exceptions, disputed usages, or odd by-ways of the language. This is something that no single book could do at any rate.

2) To be exegetical, or more properly, to provide commentary on the exegesis of various passages, disputed or not. I make every effort to keep the focus on koine as a language.

* * *

Why study the koine?

An interest in the original Greek of the Bible is what draws many people to a study of the koine, and all language study has its benefits. Still, the Greek of the New Testament offers several particular advantages to individuals who wish to achieve some proficiency in another language.

It is well-studied, with a surfeit of resources and texts available to the learner, including dictionaries and translations available without cost on the internet.

A basic competence can be acquired by book, with the focus on learning to read, and with little time spent on understanding Greek by ear, or speaking it. (Although see my notes on pronunciation, below.)

In some cases--a modest number, perhaps, but still helpful--the koine word looks and sounds like the related English word; see, for example, the koine for 'prophet', 'apostle', 'martyr', and 'lamp'.

The vocabulary as a whole is limited--some 5400 plus words--and the New Testament contains a fixed number of discrete sentences. A student of the koine will never stand in a crowded Athens shop, searching for a reply to the friendly torrent of Greek which has just greeted his attempt at "Good morning."

This last, of course, is also its weakness. Greek is a living language, but the koine dialect--despite its considerable similarity to the modern tongue--is not so. No native speakers of the koine are alive today to give the student insight into usage and idiom. We must rely on scholars for our understanding of detail.

How should I go about beginning my study of New Testament Greek?

The first step is to learn the Greek alphabet, which has some letters in common with the Latin-based alphabet of English, but not enough to make life easy. The first words can be acquired in conjunction with mastering the alphabet; after that we proceed directly to the basic grammar of koine Greek.

Should I bother with pronunciation, or with reading passages aloud?

This will ultimately be a personal choice, but my answer as a teacher is strongly 'yes'. Human beings learn their mother tongue by ear first, and only later by eye, in reading; we function this way. A language should be heard, and it is my belief that the rhythms of the spoken word contribute to its understanding.

Ah, but which pronunciation should I use?

The debate on this topic continues to be lively. My own preference is to use the pronunciation of modern Greek when speaking koine, and I present the rules for the modern language in Lesson 1. My reasons for using this system are outlined in Appendix 2, but the same appendix also gives the most common alternate pronunciation (the 'Erasmian').

What additional books should I have at hand to use this workbook?

None are necessary in the beginning, but you may wish to purchase a Greek New Testament, or use one of the Greek New Testaments on-line. In addition, you may eventually want a more complete textbook of the koine.

As mentioned, Appendix 1 at the end of this volume gives a list of resources, and my recommendations.

* * *

The website

εν αρχή
ην
ο λόγος

The associated website for the *Workbook* series is found at

http://koineworkbook.wordpress.com/

This website includes sound files for the exercises in this book, and links to other Greek language and New Testament resources on the web. Throughout this book the icon above (εν αρχή ην ο λόγος - 'in the beginning was the word') indicates an associated sound file.

Errata discovered by myself or by readers will also be noted immediately on the website.

* * *

LESSON 1 _____

The twenty-four letters of the koine Greek alphabet, and a quick guide to their modern Greek pronunciation

a. The letters

Here are the upper and lower case letters, from A (alpha) to Ω (omega), and their names in Greek, with English transliteration.

A	α	ἄλφα	alpha
B	β	βῆτα	beta
Γ	γ	γάμμα	gamma
Δ	δ	δέλτα	delta
E	ε	ἐ ψιλόν	epsilon
Z	ζ	ζῆτα	zeta
H	η	ἦτα	eta
Θ	θ	θῆτα	theta
I	ι	ἰῶτα	iota
K	κ	κάππα	kappa
Λ	λ	λάμβδα	lambda
M	μ	μῦ	mi
N	ν	νῦ	ni
Ξ	ξ	ξῖ	xi
O	ο	ὂ μικρόν	omicron ("o-small")
Π	π	πῖ	pi
P	ϱ	ῥῶ	rho
Σ	σ,ς	σίγμα	sigma
T	τ	ταῦ	tau
Υ	υ	ὖ ψιλόν	upsilon
Φ	φ	φῖ	phi
X	χ	χῖ	chi

| Ψ | ψ | ψῖ | psi |
| Ω | ω | ὦ μέγα | omega ("o-big") |

* * *

Note that 'sigma' has three forms: the capital 'Σ', the lowercase 'σ' used at the beginning or in the middle of a word, and the lowercase 'ς' used only at the end of a word.

- Examples:

  Σάρρα ('Sarah') -- capital sigma

  στολή ('robe') -- lowercase sigma used at the beginning of a word

  Ἰσραήλ ('Israel') -- lowercase sigma used in the middle of a word

  βίβλος ('book') -- lowercase sigma used at the end of a word

'Sigma' is found in two other forms as well: 'C' (capital) and 'c' (lowercase), called the lunate sigma because of their crescent shape.

The lunate forms were known from antiquity, and are found in many uncial manuscripts of the New Testament (see Fig. 1). In addition, they are not uncommon in religious contexts in modern Greece (as a decorative font, inscriptions on churches, etc.) However, they are normally not used in modern printed texts of the New Testament[1] and we may put them aside.

* * *

---

[1] Although I have found one otherwise useful on-line interlinear New Testament (at the scripture4all.org website) which uses both all capital letters for the Greek *and* the lunate sigma: thus in John 1 we find ΕΝ ΑΡΧΗ ΗΝ Ο ΛΟΓΟC.

EXERCISE 1-1: Writing Greek letters. Even if your goal is only to read New Testament Greek you may find value in practicing the written alphabet; forming the letters by hand provides a familiarity that will greatly assist in recognizing those same letters by eye.

Note that some letters present very little problem for the English speaker: kappa (K, κ), omicron (O, o), and tau (T, τ), for example, look and sound very similar to the corresponding English letter.

Other letters such as xi (Ξ, ξ) and psi (Ψ, ψ) are so different as to require practice in writing, but are unlikely to be mistaken for anything else.

The most confusing, however, are the letters that we think we know, but do not. Pay particular attention to

     (1) rho (P, ϱ), which is often mistaken for p (πι), and

     (2) ni (N, ν), which is easily recognized in the uppercase, but looks in the lowercase like the English 'v' (i.e., v as in very).

I suggest focusing below on the lowercase letters. Some of the example letters have arrows to indicate the beginning or the direction of a stroke, as seemed most useful.

α   β   γ   δ   ε   ζ

A α _____

B β _____

Γ γ _____

Δ δ _____

Ε ε _____

Ζ ζ _____

_____

η θ ι κ λ μ

Η η _____

Θ θ _____

Ι ι _____

K κ   _____

Λ λ   _____

M μ   _____

         _____

ν   ξ   ο $\vec{\pi}$ ρ   σ ς

N ν   _____

Ξ ξ   _____

O ο   _____

Π π   _____

P ϱ _____

Σ σ ς _____

_____

τ   ↓υ   ↓φ   χ   ↳ψ   ↓ω

T τ _____

Υ υ _____

Φ φ _____

Χ χ _____

Ψ ψ _____

Ω ω _____

_____

_____

EXERCISE 1-1, continued: Write out the Greek alphabet (in lower case only) in the proper order. There are 24 letters.

_____

_____

_____

α β γ δ ε ζ η θ ι κ λ μ ν ξ ο π ρ σ τ υ φ χ ψ ω

* * *

b. Pronunciation 1:
The sounds

The pronunciation rules of modern Greek are not as complicated as those of English; what you see is often what you get. Below is a basic guide, with each sound matched as closely as possible to a sound in English.

Single letters are given first, followed by an abbreviated description of certain vowel and consonant combinations.

Despite my preference for the modern system, I must add that if the reader is using this book in preparation for a university or seminary class in koine, it would be a good idea to inquire as to the pronunciation employed, and to adjust accordingly. The rules for the standard, academic Erasmian pronunciation can be found in Appendix 2.

SINGLE LETTERS

A	α	ἄλφα	ah, as in father
B	β	βῆτα	v, as in very
Γ	γ	γάμμα	(1) when before an 'e' or an 'i' sound, somewhat like y, as in yes
			(2) when before an 'a' or an 'o' sound, or another consonant, somewhat like the g in ago, but softer ('gh')
			(3) when doubled (γγ), 'ng' as in finger
Δ	δ	δέλτα	th, as in then, there - the softer 'th' sound
E	ε	ἐ ψιλόν	e, as in met - a short 'e'
Z	ζ	ζῆτα	z, as in zebra
H	η	ἦτα	i, as in machine, or a shorter 'ee' in meet
Θ	θ	θῆτα	th, as in think, thin - the harder 'th' sound
I	ι	ἰῶτα	i, as in machine, or a shorter 'ee' in meet (the same as η)
K	κ	κάππα	k, as in keep
Λ	λ	λάμβδα	l, as in let
M	μ	μῦ	m, as in man

Ν	ν	νῦ	n, as in never
Ξ	ξ	ξῖ	x, as in taxi
Ο	ο	ὂ μικρόν	o, as in oval
Π	π	πῖ	p, as in Peter
Ρ	ϱ	ῥῶ	r, as in room, except the Greek r can be slightly rolled
Σ	σ,ς	σίγμα	s, as in sea
Τ	τ	ταῦ	t, as in tea
Υ	υ	ὖ ψιλόν	i, as in machine, or a shorter 'ee' in meet (the same as η and ι)
Φ	φ	φῖ	f, as in fun
Χ	χ	χῖ	somewhat like the 'h' in hue, or ch as in German 'Bach'
Ψ	ψ	ψῖ	ps, as in maps
Ω	ω	ὦ μέγα	o, as in oval; the same sound as omicron

Note that the sound of each letter is found in its Greek name, so that by practicing the alphabet you also learn pronunciation. I can recommend reciting the alphabet in groups of five, with a final group of four. A sound file of the alphabet is found on the accompanying website.[1]

εν αρχή
ην
ο λόγος

* * *

VOWEL COMBINATIONS: αι, ει, οι, ου, αυ, and ευ

1. **αι**

   The combination 'αι' is pronounced like the Greek vowel 'ε'; i.e., 'e' as in met

2. **ει, οι**

   The combinations 'ει ' and 'οι ' are both pronounced like 'η', 'ι', and 'υ'. This means that there are a total of five vowels or vowel combinations that have the same pronunciation (i.e., as the i in machine, or a shorter 'ee' in meet).

---

[1] http://koineworkbook.wordpress.com/ (see Introduction)

3. ου

The combination 'ου' is pronounced as the ou in soup.

4. αυ

The combination 'αυ' is pronounced as 'ahf' or 'ahv'

- Examples:

  ταῦτα = TAHFta ('these things')

  Παῦλος = PAHVlos ('Paul')

'ahf' when this combination comes at the end of a word, or when it precedes these consonants:
π, τ, κ, φ, θ, χ, σ, ξ, ψ

'ahv' before a vowel or any other consonant:
β, δ, γ, ζ, λ, ρ, μ, ν

Also note that the name of the letter 'τ' (ταυ) is pronounced 'tahf',

5. ευ

Similarly, the combination 'ευ' is pronounced 'ef' or 'ev'

- Examples:

  δεύτερος = THEFteros ('second')

  βασιλεύω = vasiLEVo ('I rule')

'ef' when this combination comes at the end of a word, or when it precedes these consonants:
π, τ, κ, φ, θ, χ, σ, ξ, ψ

'ev' before a vowel or any other consonant:
β, δ, γ, ζ, λ, ρ, μ, ν

CONSONANT COMBINATIONS: μπ, ντ, and

1. The combination '**μπ**' is generally pronounced as 'mb' in number.

- Example: ἔμπορος = EMboros ('merchant')

2. The combination '**ντ**' is pronounced as 'nd' in India.

- Example: ἐντολή = endoLEE ('commandment')

3. The combination 'γκ' is generally pronounced as 'ng' in finger. This is the same pronunciation as the double 'γγ'.

- Example: ἄγκυρα = AHNGeera ('anchor')

Mastery of the rules above may seem daunting, but the Greek language is worth the effort; consistent practice will be rewarded, and the results are quite beautiful.

* * *

EXERCISE 1-2: Practice saying the following koine words out loud. Some words will sound familiar to an English speaker. Two sound files are available on my website to check your pronunciation; one with the Greek words only, and one including an English equivalent for each word.

εν αρχή
ην
ο λόγος

Μαγδαληνή	Ἀπολλῶς
προφήτης	γλῶσσα
ἀπόστολος	γράφω
Μάρθα	δράκων
Μαρία	ἐκκλησία
ἐπιστολή	ζωή
Ζαχαρίας	θεός
Ἱεροσόλυμα	Ἰησοῦς
καλέω	Λάζαρος
ὀφθαλμός	Πιλᾶτος
μαθητής	πέντε
ἄγγελος	ἀγάπη

* * *

The Lord's Prayer

εν αρχή
ην
ο λόγος

I have included--on the website--a sound file of the Lord's Prayer read in koine Greek, using the modern pronunciation. The passage being read is below; it is taken from the Byzantine Majority text (see Appendix 1) and differs from other standard readings only in the verb form ἀφίεμεν. On the right is a rough word for word translation.

Πάτερ ἡμῶν ὁ ἐν τοῖς οὐρανοῖς·	Father our he in the heavens
ἁγιασθήτω τὸ ὄνομά σου·	let it be holy the name yours
ἐλθέτω ἡ βασιλεία σου·	let it come the kingdom yours
γενηθήτω τὸ θέλημά σου,	let it happen the will yours
ὡς ἐν οὐρανῷ καὶ ἐπὶ τῆς γῆς·	as in heaven and on the earth
τὸν ἄρτον ἡμῶν τὸν ἐπιούσιον	the bread ours the necessary/daily
δὸς ἡμῖν σήμερον·	give to us today
καὶ ἄφες ἡμῖν τὰ ὀφειλήματα ἡμῶν,	and forgive us the debts ours
ὡς καὶ ἡμεῖς ἀφίεμεν τοῖς ὀφειλέταις ἡμῶν·	as also we forgive the debtors ours
καὶ μὴ εἰσενέγκης ἡμᾶς εἰς πειρασμόν,	and not lead us into temptation
ἀλλὰ ῥῦσαι ἡμᾶς ἀπὸ τοῦ πονηροῦ.	but deliver us from the evil one

Matthew 6: 9-13

* * *

c. Pronunciation 2:
Accents and breathing marks

Printed koine Greek uses a system of three accent marks and two breathing marks. The accents are the acute, the grave, and the circumflex, as follows:

Πέτρος (acute)   Peter

Παῦλος (circumflex)   Paul

Πέτρος καὶ Παῦλος (acute, grave, circumflex)   Peter and Paul

Each Greek word usually receives one accent, which cannot fall further than three syllables from the end of the word. Although there are more rules defining the circumstances in which each accent is used, all three are pronounced identically, as a simple stress accent (e.g., ΠΕΤρος, PEter). A student need only take account of the position.

Breathing marks (rough breathing as in ἁ, smooth breathing as in ἀ) are included over every vowel which begins a word (e.g., ἐπιστολή, letter). In addition, the mark for rough breathing is used over a word-initial rho (e.g., ῥαββί, rabbi). They do not affect the modern Greek pronunciation in any way, and will not be considered further.

It should be noted that neither accents nor breathing marks were included in the earliest Greek manuscripts of the New Testament. See Fig. 1 for a fourth century example.

* * *

EXERCISE 1-3: Practice saying these koine words and phrases out loud. Check your pronunciation using the website sound file for this exercise.

 εν αρχή
ην
ο λόγος

koine	word-for-word (as best possible)	a standard translation
ἐγράφη	it was written	it was written
εὐχαριστῶ	I thank	I thank
ἀδελφοί	brothers	brothers
ἀκούομεν	we hear	we hear
ποιήσομεν	we will do	we will do
ἐν ἀρχῇ ἦν ὁ λόγος	in beginning was the word	in the beginning was the word
ὁ θεὸς φῶς ἐστιν	the God light is	God is light
ἄνθρωπος ἦν	man was	there was a man
φέρετέ μοι δηνάριον	bring me denarius	bring me a denarius
ἔρχονται εἰς χωρίον	they come/go to place	they went to a place
εἰς τὴν ἔρημον	into the wilderness	into the wilderness
ἐν τῇ σκοτίᾳ	in the darkness	in the darkness
σὺ εἶ ὁ διδάσκαλος	you are the teacher	you are the teacher

LESSON 2 _____

Introduction to the Greek verb

a. Preliminary notes

Greek verbs are conjugated. That is, they change form (i.e., spelling) according to:

> person[1] (first, second, or third),
> number (singular or plural),
> tense (past, present and future, roughly),
> voice[2] (active, middle, passive), and
> mood[3] (indicative, subjunctive, imperative, optative),

- Examples:

> εὑρίσκω - I find; 1st person, singular, present tense,
> active voice, indicative mood

> εὑρήσεις - you will find; 2nd person, singular, future tense,
> active voice, indicative mood

The participle and infinitive are also verb forms, and have their own roles in a complete verb conjugation; they will be considered later, at some length.

_____

[1] I and we = first person; you (singular and plural) = second person; he, she, it, they = third person

[2] I find = active voice; I am found = passive voice. The middle voice is a Greek peculiarity to be covered later.

[3] To be covered in later volumes of the *Workbook* series.

English verbs are conjugated as well. The conjugation of the English verb, however, is not as complete--or perhaps it would be more accurate to say, not as visible--as that of the Greek. The verb 'find', for example, is the same form (spelling) for most persons and numbers of the present tense: I find, you find, we find, they find (although she *finds*). Only the subject of the verb (I, you, we, they) makes the person and number clear.

* * *

b. Morphology of the present tense

The present tense of βλέπω (I see) consists of the root (βλέπ-), combined with tense endings indicating person and number (-ω, -εις, -ει, -ομεν, -ετε, -ουσι(ν)).

εν αρχή
ην
ο λόγος

Table 2-1: Verb morphology: Present active indicative of βλέπω

βλέπω	I see	βλέπομεν	we see
βλέπεις	you (sing.) see	βλέπετε	you (pl.) see
βλέπει	he/she/it sees	βλέπουσι(ν)*	they see

*The third person plural has alternative spellings; either with or without a final 'ν'.

Note: Verb conjugations will regularly be displayed as above, in two columns with the singular to the left and the plural to the right. 'Sing.' (singular) and 'pl.' (plural) will be omitted in future sections unless needed for clarification.

Examples of other verbs which are conjugated like (i.e., have the same endings as) βλέπω:

γράφω (I write)   διδάσκω (I teach)
ἀναβαίνω (I go up)   πίνω (I drink)
λέγω (I say)   ἔχω (I have)

* * *

EXERCISE 2-1: Cover the right column, and translate. Uncover to check your answers. For further work retranslate the English back to Greek using the final column.

 εν αρχή
ην
ο λόγος

βλέπω   _____   I see _____

γράφεις   _____   you write (sing.) _____

διδάσκει   _____   he/she/it teaches _____

ἔχομεν   _____   we have _____

γράφετε _____ you write (pl.) _____

ἀναβαίνω _____ I go up _____

πίνουσιν _____ they drink _____

γράφουσι _____ they write _____

λέγεις _____ you say (sing.) _____

διδάσκετε _____ you teach (pl.) _____

βλέπομεν _____ we see _____

EXERCISE 2-2: Write out the complete conjugation of the verbs γράφω and διδάσκω in the present tense.

εν αρχή
ην
ο λόγος

_____ _____ γράφω   γράφομεν

_____ _____ γράφεις γράφετε

_____ _____ γράφει   γράφουσι(ν)

		διδάσκω	διδάσκομεν
_____	_____	διδάσκεις	διδάσκετε
_____	_____	διδάσκει	διδάσκουσι(ν)

* * *

c. Additional notes

Separate words for 'I', 'you', 'she', etc., are generally not *obligatory* as the subject of a verb in Greek; βλέπω means 'I see', not 'see'.

The personal pronouns exist, but their inclusion as the subject is often for emphasis or contrast.

- Examples:

ἐγώ = I	Ἐγὼ δὲ λέγω	But I say	Matthew 5: 22
σύ = you, sing.	Σὺ λέγεις	You say [it]	Mark 15: 2
ἡμεῖς = we	καὶ **ἡμεῖς** ἀλλαγησόμεθα	and we will be changed	1 Cor. 15: 52

EXERCISE 2-3: Give the third person singular for the verbs below.

διδάσκω (teach) ＿＿＿＿＿＿＿＿＿＿ διδάσκει

γράφω (write) ＿＿＿＿＿＿＿＿＿＿ γράφει

λέγω (say) ＿＿＿＿＿＿＿＿＿＿ λέγει

ἀναβαίνω (go up) ＿＿＿＿＿＿＿＿＿＿ ἀναβαίνει

βλέπω (see) ＿＿＿＿＿＿＿＿＿＿ βλέπει

ἔχω (have) ＿＿＿＿＿＿＿＿＿＿ ἔχει

EXERCISE 2-4: Give the second person plural for the verbs below:

πίνω (drink) ＿＿＿＿＿＿＿＿＿＿ πίνετε

ἔχω (have) ＿＿＿＿＿＿＿＿＿＿ ἔχετε

βλέπω (see) ＿＿＿＿＿＿＿＿＿＿ βλέπετε

διδάσκω (teach)   _____   διδάσκετε

λέγω (say)   _____   λέγετε

ἀναβαίνω (go up)   _____   ἀναβαίνετε

ἔχω (have)   _____   ἔχετε

* * *

EXERCISE 2-5: Give the third person plural for the verbs below and translate the third person form:

λέγω   _____   λέγουσι(ν) they say

γράφω   _____   γράφουσι(ν) they write

ἀναβαίνω   _____   ἀναβαίνουσι(ν) they go up

βλέπω   _____   βλέπουσι(ν) they see

* * *

LESSON 3 _____

Introduction to the Greek noun
Masculine nouns, second declension

a. Preliminary notes

Just as Greek verbs are conjugated, Greek nouns are declined; that is, they change form according to their function in a phrase or sentence.

English nouns are not extensively declined, although they do distinguish singular and plural (child, children) and can show possession (the child's book). In addition, parts of a declension system remain in use for English personal pronouns.

- Examples:

    I, he, we: nominative case; used for the subject of a sentence

    > **I** went to Jerusalem. **He** wrote a letter.
    > **We** taught them.

    me, him, us: accusative case; a variety of uses, including the direct object

    > He sent **me** a letter. I sent **him** a letter.
    > They taught **us**.

The system for koine Greek is more involved, and applies to almost all nouns, with exceptions for some foreign loan words.

Koine nouns are found in two numbers (singular and plural) and five cases (nominative, genitive, dative, accusative, and vocative). Koine nouns also have one of three genders: masculine, feminine, or neuter.

Thus, a common koine noun (of whatever gender) has a total of ten possible forms (see Table 3-1, below). Proper names typically have only singular forms.

Table 3-1: Noun numbers and cases

nominative singular	nominative plural
genitive singular	genitive plural
dative singular	dative plural
accusative singular	accusative plural
vocative singular*	vocative plural*

---

*The vocative case is the case of direct address (e.g., 'brother' in "Brother, come here!"). It is much less common than the other cases and will be omitted from the tables below.

Koine nouns are grouped into *declensions*, with each declension having its own pattern of endings. For our purposes, it's easiest to think of a noun as consisting of a root to which an ending is added, each ending indicating a number and case.

- Examples:

  ἀπόστολος (apostle) is formed from the root ἀποστολ- plus the case ending -ος, designating this as a nominative singular form.

  ἀπόστολοι (apostles) is formed from the root ἀποστολ- plus the case ending -οι, designating this as a nominative plural form.

ἀποστόλων (apostles', of apostles) is formed from the root ἀποστολ- plus the case ending -ων, designating this as a genitive plural form.

* * *

There are three major declensions in koine Greek, each with sub-groups and variations. We will begin with an example from the second declension.

b. Morphology of θεός, a second declension masculine noun ending in -ος

The case endings for this group begin with either an omicron (o) or an omega (ω):

-ος	nominative singular	-οι	nominative plural
-ου	genitive singular	-ων	genitive plural
-ῳ	dative singular	-οις	dative plural
-ον	accusative singular	-ους	accusative plural

In Table 3-2, then, the words are formed by combining the root θε- with the case endings given above.

εν αρχή ην ο λόγος

Table 3-2: Declension of θεός, a second declension masculine noun

nom.	θεός	a god	nom.	θεοί	gods
gen.	θεοῦ	of a god	gen.	θεῶν	of gods
dat.	θεῷ	to or for a god	dat.	θεοῖς	to or for gods
acc.	θεόν	a god	acc.	θεούς	gods

Declensions will be presented with the cases ordered as Table 3-2, with singular to the left and plural to the right.

* * *

c. Additional notes

The second declension is sometimes referred to as the 'o-declension'.

There are also neuter and (a few) feminine nouns of this declension. These nouns follow a similar declension pattern to the masculine nouns and will be covered in a later lesson.

The English equivalents given in declension tables are general and approximate. A more exact translation will depend on context.

For example, in Matthew 5: 24 the dative singular form for 'brother' (ἀδελφῷ) is usually translated using 'to':

πρῶτον διαλλάγηθι τῷ **ἀδελφῷ** σου   first be reconciled **to** your **brother**

On the other hand, in Luke 20:28, the same form is usually translated using 'for':

ἐξαναστήσῃ σπέρμα τῷ **ἀδελφῷ** αὐτοῦ   raise up offspring **for** his **brother**

And in Matthew 18:35, the same form is translated without either 'to' or 'for':

ἐὰν μὴ ἀφῆτε . . . τῷ **ἀδελφῷ** αὐτοῦ   if you do not forgive your **brother**

* * *

εν αρχή
ην
ο λόγος

Other masculine nouns with the same case endings as θεός include:

ἄνθρωπος	person, human being	υἱός	son
θρόνος	throne	θησαυρός	treasure
λόγος	word	κόσμος	world (found in singular only)
νόμος	law	ἀδελφός	brother
οὐρανός	heaven	κύριος	master, Lord
ἵππος	horse	ποταμός	river

* * *

EXERCISE 3-1: Translate each noun, using Table 3-2 as a guide. Identify the case.

Remember that the English equivalent for an isolated word can be only general and approximate. Note that 'a' is added before singular nouns in the translation key, to correspond to English usage. This indefinite article is not present in the Greek.

ἀδελφοί _____   brothers, nominative plural

οὐρανοῦ _____   of heaven, genitive singular

νόμῳ _____   to or for a law, dative singular

λόγους _____   words, accusative plural

κυρίοις _____   to or for masters, dative plural

κόσμος _____   world, nominative singular

ἵπποις   _____   to or for horses, dative plural

θησαυροῦ   _____   of a treasure, genitive singular

ποταμοί   _____   rivers, nominative plural

υἱόν   _____   son, accusative singular

***

EXERCISE 3-2: Translate the following words and short phrases.

ἀδελφὸς βλέπει _____   a brother sees

ἀδελφοὶ βλέπουσιν _____   brothers see

ἄνθρωπος βλέπει _____   a person sees

ἄνθρωποι βλέπουσι _____   persons see

βλέπομεν _____   we see

ἵππος πίνει _____   a horse drinks

ἵπποι πίνουσιν _____ horses drink

υἱὸς διδάσκει _____ a son teaches

υἱοὶ διδάσκουσι _____ sons teach

διδάσκομεν _____ we teach

κύριος γράφει _____ a master writes

γράφω _____ I write

ἀδελφοὶ γράφουσιν _____ brothers write

θησαυρὸς ἔχει _____ a treasure has

ἵππος ἔχει _____ a horse has

ἵπποι ἔχουσιν _____ horses have

* * *

LESSON 4 _____

Introduction to the Greek noun, continued
Feminine nouns, first declension

a. Preliminary notes

The gender of a Greek noun sometimes corresponds to its meaning in an obvious way, and sometimes does not.

- Examples of correspondence:

  γυνή, μήτηρ -- a woman, a mother, feminine words in Greek
  ἀνήρ, πατήρ -- a man, a father, masculine words in Greek

  proper names: The gender of a proper name (Μαρία, Mary; Ἰησοῦς, Jesus; Ἐλισάβετ, Elizabeth; Παῦλος, Paul) corresponds to the gender of the individual named.

- Examples where the gender of the word does not correspond in an obvious way:

  The word ὄχλος (crowd, multitude) is masculine, whereas the word πλῆθος (crowd, people, assembly) is neuter.

  The word κοράσιον (girl) is neuter.

  The word ἔχιδνα (snake, viper) is feminine, whereas the word ὄφις (snake, serpent) is masculine.

None of this is to say that the choice of gender for a given word is arbitrary, or without historical basis, or that there are no trends; abstract nouns, for example (hope, justice, freedom) are often feminine. But the reader must be awake to the possibility that a word's gender may not be evident at first glance.

b. Morphology of two first declension feminine nouns

εν αρχή
ην
ο λόγος

Table 4-1: Declension of καρδία, a first declension feminine noun ending in -α

nom.	καρδία	a heart		nom.	καρδίαι	hearts
gen.	καρδίας	of a heart		gen.	καρδιῶν	of hearts
dat.	καρδίᾳ	to or for a heart		dat.	καρδίαις	to or for hearts
acc.	καρδίαν	a heart		acc.	καρδίας	hearts

Table 4-2: Declension of γραφή, a first declension feminine noun ending in -η

nom.	γραφή	a writing		nom.	γραφαί	writings
gen.	γραφῆς	of a writing		gen.	γραφῶν	of writings
dat.	γραφῇ	to or for a writing		dat.	γραφαῖς	to or for writings
acc.	γραφήν	a writing		acc.	γραφάς	writings

c. Additional notes

The first declension is sometimes referred to as the 'α-declension'.

Feminine first declension nouns end in either -α or -η in the nominative singular. Those like καρδία keep the α throughout the singular of the declension. Those like γραφή keep the η.

Other feminine first declension nouns have α in the nominative and accusative singular, but η in the genitive and dative singular. All groups of feminine first declension nouns have the same endings in the plural.

Other feminine nouns like καρδία, with α throughout the singular:

εν αρχή
ην
ο λόγος

ὥρα	hour	ἐξουσία	power, authority
ἡμέρα	day	βασιλεία	kingdom
ἐκκλησία	church, assembly	ἀλήθεια	truth
ἐπαγγελία	promise	οἰκία	house

Note that the genitive singular and the accusative plural are the same form (spelling) for this sub-group of first declension nouns. See Table 4-1 and compare to Table 4-2.

Other feminine nouns like γραφή, with η throughout the singular:

παραβολή	parable	ἐντολή	commandment
κεφαλή	head	διδαχή	teaching
ἀγάπη	love	πύλη	gate
ζωή	life	ἀρχή	beginning

<u>Accents</u>: There are some variations in accent in this declension due to the historical distinction between long and short vowels. We find, for example:

$$\beta\alpha\sigma\iota\lambda\varepsilon\acute{\iota}\alpha \text{ ('kingdom', nominative), and } \beta\alpha\sigma\iota\lambda\varepsilon\acute{\iota}\alpha\varsigma \text{ (genitive)}$$

but

$$\dot{\alpha}\lambda\acute{\eta}\theta\varepsilon\iota\alpha \text{ ('truth', nominative) and } \dot{\alpha}\lambda\eta\theta\varepsilon\acute{\iota}\alpha\varsigma \text{ (genitive)}$$

These variations make the Greek spelling more difficult to predict, but not to read, and need only be noted as they occur.

* * *

EXERCISE 4-1: Translate each noun, using Tables 4-1 and 4-2 as a guide. Identify the case. Remember that the English equivalent for an isolated word can be only general and approximate.

γραφαί   _____   writings, nominative plural

παραβολή   _____   parable, nominative singular

καρδία   _____   to or for a heart, dative singular

ἐκκλησίαν   _____   church, accusative singular

ὥραις   _____   to or for hours, dative plural

γραφῶν   _____   of writings, genitive plural

ἐξουσία _____ authority, nominative singular

πύλας _____ gates, accusative plural

ἐντολαί _____ commandments, nom. plural

βασιλείαν _____ kingdom, accusative singular

κεφαλῶν _____ of heads, genitive plural

ἡμέρας _____ of a day, genitive singular *or*
days, accusative plural

EXERCISE 4-2: Translate, then give the accusative plural for each of the following first declension nouns:

πύλη _____ gate, πύλας

ἐκκλησία _____ church, ἐκκλησίας

ἐντολή _____ commandment, ἐντολάς

γραφή _____ writing, γραφάς

διδαχή _____ teaching, διδαχάς

EXERCISE 4-3: Write out the declension for the first declension nouns ἡμέρα (day) and
ζωή (life); in both singular and plural for ἡμέρα and in singular only for ζωή:

_____   _____   ἡμέρα   ἡμέραι

_____   _____   ἡμέρας   ἡμερῶν

_____   _____   ἡμέρᾳ   ἡμέραις

_____   _____   ἡμέραν   ἡμέρας

_____   ζωή

_____   ζωῆς

_____   ζωῇ

_____   ζωήν

Accents: Note the accent shift in the genitive plural. In the genitive plural, all first
declension nouns have a circumflex accent on the final syllable, e.g., ἡμερῶν, κεφαλῶν,
γραφῶν, ὡρῶν.

The plural forms of ζωή are not used in the New Testament.

EXERCISE 4-4: Translate and give the indicated form for each noun:

'life' in the nominative singular _____   ζωή

'commandment' in the genitive singular _____   ἐντολῆς

'parable' in the dative singular _____   παραβολῇ

'day' in the accusative singular _____   ἡμέραν

'kingdom' in the nominative plural _____   βασιλείαι

'writing' in the genitive plural _____   γραφῶν

'hour' in the dative plural _____   ὥραις

'gate' in the accusative plural _____   πύλας

LESSON 5 _____

Introduction to the use of the nominative and accusative case

a. Preliminary notes

Consider this sentence: The dog chases the cat.

The dog is the animal who chases, and is the *subject* of the sentence. In Greek, the subject of a sentence is put in the nominative case.

The cat is the animal being chased, and is the *direct object* of the verb 'chases'; i.e., 'the cat' answers the question "What does the dog chase?" In Greek, the direct object of a verb is often put in the accusative case.

- Example of the nominative case of θεός (god) used for a subject:

ὁ **θεὸς** ἠγάπησεν ἡμᾶς
[the] **God** loved us

1 John 4:11

- Example of the accusative case of θεός used for the direct object:

ἡμεῖς ἠγαπήκαμεν τὸν **θεόν**
we have loved [the] **God**

1 John 4:10

b. Accusative morphology

The table below summarizes the accusative endings for the declension groups we have learned so far, with examples.

Table 5-1: The accusative endings for 2nd declension, masculine, and 1st declension, feminine, words

masculine, singular accusative	-ον	ἄνθρωπον
masculine, plural accusative	-ους	ἀνθρώπους
feminine, singular accusative	-ην	γραφήν
	-αν	ἐκκλησίαν
feminine, plural accusative	-ας	ἐκκλησίας

EXERCISE 5:1 Translate the following phrases. Identify which nouns are in the nominative, and which in the accusative case.

ἄνθρωπος βλέπει ἵππον _____ a person sees a horse

ἄνθρωποι βλέπουσιν ἵππους _____ people see horses

ἵππος βλέπει ἄνθρωπον _____ a horse sees a
person

ἵππος βλέπει ἀνθρώπους _____ a horse sees
people

ἄνθρωπος διδάσκει ἵππον _____ a person teaches
a horse

ἄνθρωποι διδάσκουσιν ἵππους _____ people teach horses

ἄνθρωπος γράφει ἐντολήν _____ a person writes a
commandment

ἄνθρωποι γράφουσιν ἐντολάς _____ people write
commandments

In all cases above, the first noun in the phrase is in the nominative case, and is the subject of the phrase. The second noun is in the accusative case, and is the direct object of the verb.

* * *

EXERCISE 5-2: Translate the following phrases. Identify which nouns are in the nominative, and which in the accusative case.

ἄνθρωπον βλέπει ἵππος _____ a horse sees a person

ἀνθρώπους βλέπουσιν ἵπποι _____ horses see people

ἵππον βλέπει ἄνθρωπος _____ a person sees a horse

ἵππον βλέπουσιν ἄνθρωποι _____ people see a horse

ἄνθρωπον διδάσκει ἵππος _____ a horse teaches a person

ἀνθρώπους διδάσκουσιν ἵπποι _____ horses teach people

* * *

c. Additional notes

Not *all* direct objects are expressed with the accusative, depending to some extent on the nature of the verb. The verb βλέπω, for example, regularly takes an accusative direct object (βλέπω ἵππον - I see a horse), but the verb πιστεύω (I believe, trust) takes a dative object: πιστεύω τῷ λόγῳ - I believe the word.

* * *

Notice the difference between the first phrase in Exercise 5-1:

ἄνθρωπος βλέπει ἵππον   a person sees a horse

and the first phrase in Exercise 5-2:

ἄνθρωπον βλέπει ἵππος   a horse sees a person

In each case the word order is the same in Greek; the word for 'person' comes first, then the verb, then the word for 'horse'. But the meaning of the two phrases is *not* the same; a person seeing a horse is not the same as a horse seeing a person.

What has happened here? We have changed the case of the nouns. In the first example the word ἄνθρωπος is in the nominative case, so that wherever it is found within this phrase, it must be the subject. The word ἵππον is in the accusative case, so it must be the direct object.

Similarly for the word ἵππος in the second phrase; it is in the nominative case and must therefore be the subject. The word ἄνθρωπον is accusative, and must be the direct object.

In other words, unlike the case in English, word order in Greek is flexible.
The standard order in an English phrase is subject-verb-object, so that if we want to say *the cat chases the dog*, 'the cat' must come first. In Greek the order can be *the dog chases the cat*--and still mean *the cat chases the dog*!--as long as 'the cat' is kept in the nominative case, and 'dog' in the accusative.

- Examples:

    1.   ἀδελφὸς βλέπει ἄνθρωπον   a brother sees a person

means basically the same thing as

ἄνθρωπον βλέπει ἀδελφός   a brother sees a person

2.   ἄνθρωπος γράφει ἐντολήν   a person writes a commandment

means basically the same thing as

ἐντολὴν γράφει ἄνθρωπος   a person writes a commandment

* * *

I have gone into some detail here because this aspect of Greek is an obstacle for English speakers. We tend to start at the beginning of a sentence and translate from there, assuming that whatever noun we run into first must be the subject. This is not true in Greek, and you will save yourself a great deal of trouble if you focus first on identifying the subject of every verb, regardless of its position in the sentence.

* * *

EXERCISE 5-3: Identify (only) the subject of these phrases. You should be able to do this without understanding the entire meaning of the phrase, but I have given a translation in the key below. The phrases are from the New Testament; some are slightly adapted.

1. ἐὰν ἁμαρτήσῃ ὁ ἀδελφός σου   subject:_____

    subject: ἀδελφός (brother)
    translation: if your brother sins
    word for word translation (as best possible):
                ἐὰν ἁμαρτήσῃ ὁ ἀδελφός σου
                if   sins   the brother of you

2. ἔφθασεν ἡ βασιλεία τοῦ θεοῦ   subject:_____

      subject: βασιλεία (kingdom)
      translation: the kingdom of God has come
      word for word translation:
            ἔφθασεν ἡ βασιλεία τοῦ θεοῦ
            has come the kingdom of [the] God

3. ὁ κόσμος αὐτὸν οὐκ ἔγνω   subject:_____

      subject: κόσμος (world)
      translation: the world did not know him
      word for word translation:
            ὁ κόσμος αὐτὸν οὐκ ἔγνω
            the world him   not did know

4. συνέλθῃ ἡ ἐκκλησία ὅλη   subject:_____

      subject: ἐκκλησία
      translation: the whole church comes together
      word for word translation:
            συνέλθῃ   ἡ ἐκκλησία ὅλη
            comes together   the church   whole

* * *

LESSON 6 _____

The article

a. Preliminary notes

You may have noticed that there was a short word (ὁ or ἡ) preceding each subject in Exercise 5-3. These short words are the article, i.e., 'the'.

ὁ ἀδελφός   the brother

ἡ βασιλεία   the kingdom

ὁ κόσμος   the world

In Greek, the article is declined--just like nouns--according to gender, case, and number.

- Examples: ὁ ἄνθρωπος   the person   (masculine, nominative, singular)

    ἡ ζωή   the life   (feminine, nominative, singular)

    τοῦ ἀνθρώπου   of the person (masculine, genitive, singular)

    τῆς ζωῆς   of the life   (feminine, genitive, singular)

We have not seen any neuter nouns yet, but the nominative form for the singular neuter article is τό:

τὸ δῶρον   the gift

τὸ ἔργον   the work, deed

Neuter nouns will be addressed at more length in the next lesson.

* * *

The Greek article is used in a manner roughly--but only roughly--equivalent to the English definite article. That is, you will *often* see it in Greek when you would expect to see 'the' in English.

- Example: τὸ φῶς ἐν τῇ σκοτίᾳ φαίνει
  the light in **the** darkness shines
  the light shines in the darkness   John 1:5

However, differences exist. One notable one is the use of the article with 'θεός'; Greek often says 'the god' when English says 'God'.

- Example: τίς δύναται ἁμαρτίας ἀφεῖναι εἰ μὴ μόνος ὁ θεός;
  who is able sins to forgive except alone [the] god
  Who can forgive sins but God alone?   Luke 5: 21

In addition, Greek often uses the article before proper names.

- Examples: εἶπεν ὁ Ἰησοῦς
  said [the] Jesus
  Jesus said

  ἀνεῦραν τήν τε Μαριὰμ καὶ τὸν Ἰωσήφ
  they found [the] Mary and [the] Joseph
  they found Mary and Joseph   Luke 2: 16

* * *

Other major differences between Greek and English usage of the article will be noted as they occur.

b. Morphology of the article

Table 6-1: Forms of the article

	singular			plural		
	masculine	feminine	neuter	masculine	feminine	neuter
nom.	ὁ	ἡ	τό	οἱ	αἱ	τά
gen.	τοῦ	τῆς	τοῦ	τῶν	τῶν	τῶν
dat.	τῷ	τῇ	τῷ	τοῖς	ταῖς	τοῖς
acc.	τόν	τήν	τό	τούς	τάς	τά

Note that (1) all forms other than the masculine and feminine nominatives begin with 'τ', (2) the neuter nominative and accusative are identical, (3) the neuter genitive and dative forms are identical to the masculine forms, and (4) all the genitive plurals are the same.

EXERCISE 6-1: Using the table above, give the form of the article that would accompany each of the following masculine or feminine nouns.

εν αρχή
ην
ο λόγος

_____ ἄνθρωπος   _____ ἀδελφός   ὁ, ὁ

_____ ἀνθρώπου   _____ ἀδελφοῦ   τοῦ, τοῦ

_____ ἄνθρωποι   _____ ἀδελφοί   οἱ, οἱ

_____ βασιλεία   _____ ἐντολή   ἡ, ἡ

_____ παραβολαῖς   _____ ἐντολῆς   ταῖς, τῆς

_____ λόγῳ   _____ λόγοις   τῷ, τοῖς

_____ ἐπαγγελίαν   _____ ἐπαγγελίας   τήν, τῆς or τάς*

_____ ποταμούς   _____ ποταμόν   τούς, τόν

*The noun form ἐπαγγελίας could be either genitive singular or accusative plural.

* * *

EXERCISE 6-2: Translate from the Greek. Identify case and number.

οἱ λόγοι _____   the words   nominative plural

τοῦ λόγου _____   of the word   genitive singular

ἡ ἐκκλησία _____   the church   nominative singular

τοὺς νόμους _____   the laws   accusative plural

τῇ ζωῇ _____   to or for the life   dative singular

τὰς παραβολάς _____   the parables   accusative plural

τοῖς ἀδελφοῖς _____   to or for the brothers   dative plural

αἱ ἡμέραι _____   the days   nominative plural

τῶν ὡρῶν _____   of the hours genitive plural

ὁ θρόνος τοῦ θεοῦ _____   the throne of [the] God
                                                 nominative singular, genitive singular

EXERCISE 6-3: Translate from the Greek. Answers are grouped at the end.

1. ὁ ἄνθρωπος βλέπει τὸν ποταμόν. _____

2. ὁ ἀδελφὸς γράφει τὰς εντολάς. _____

3. οἱ ἄνθρωποι λέγουσι τοὺς λόγους. _____

4. οἱ ἀδελφοί διδάσκουσιν τοὺς ἵππους. _____

5. ὁ θεὸς ἔχει τὴν ἐξουσία. _____

1. The man sees the river.
2. The brother writes the commandments.
3. The men say the words.
4. The brothers teach the horses.
5. [The] God has the authority.

c. Additional notes

Although proper accentuation is important for fluency in reading koine Greek out loud, neither accents nor breathing marks will normally affect meaning or ease of understanding. A longer word such as ἄνθρωπος or ἐκκλησία, for example, is just as likely to be recognized with or without these additions.

But for some of the very short words--including the article--accents and breathing marks (and the iota subscript) do affect meaning and should be carefully noted. Notice first that the article forms ὁ, ἡ, οἱ, and αἱ have only breathing marks; these words are *proclitics*, which means that they are considered to be so closely associated with the following word that they have no accent of their own. But there are other, similar words that do have accents.

- Example: ἡ (no accent, rough breathing) is the feminine nominative singular article, but

  ἤ, ἢ (acute or grave accent, smooth breathing) is the particle meaning 'or', and

  ᾖ (circumflex accent, smooth breathing, iota subscript) is a singular subjunctive form of the verb 'to be'.

- Example: ὁ (no accent, rough breathing) is the masculine nominative singular article, but

  ὅ (acute or grave accent, rough breathing) is the neuter nominative or accusative singular relative pronoun.

* * *

LESSON 7 _____

Introduction to the Greek noun, continued
Neuter nouns of the second declension

a. Preliminary notes

Neuter nouns of the second declension share some of their endings with masculine nouns of the second declension. However, there is a key difference for this group as opposed to all other nouns: neuter nouns have identical forms for the nominative and accusative cases, both in the singular and the plural. This rule holds for any accompanying article as well. Thus we have τὸ δῶρον (the gift, neuter nominative singular) and τὸ δῶρον (the gift, neuter accusative singular). In translating the choice between nominative and accusative must be made on the basis of overall context.

εν αρχή
ην
ο λόγος

b. Morphology of second declension neuter nouns

Table 7-1: Declension of δῶρον, a second declension neuter noun, together with its article

nom.	τὸ δῶρον	the gift	nom.	τὰ δῶρα	the gifts
gen.	τοῦ δώρου	of the gift	gen.	τῶν δώρων	of the gifts
dat.	τῷ δώρῳ	to or for the gift	dat.	τοῖς δώροις	to or for the gifts
acc.	τὸ δῶρον	the gift	acc.	τὰ δῶρα	the gifts

Note the correspondence between nominative and accusative forms. Note also that the genitive and dative forms (for both the noun itself and the article) are identical to the forms for masculine second declension nouns.

Other neuter nouns of the second declension include:

		εν αρχή
		ην
		ο λόγος

τὸ ἱερόν   the temple
τὸ τέκνον   the child
τὸ ἔργον   the work, the deed
τὸ εὐαγγέλιον   the gospel

There are additional neuter nouns taken from Latin, e.g.:

τὸ μίλιον   the (Roman) mile
τὸ δηνάριον   the denarius (Roman coin)

* * *

EXERCISE 7-1: Translate from the Greek. Identify number and case for each noun.

τὰ ἔργα _____   the works/deeds   nom. or acc. plural

τοῖς τέκνοις _____   to or for the children   dative plural

τὸ ἱερόν _____   the temple   nom. or acc. singular

τὸ εὐαγγέλιον _____   the gospel   nom. or acc. singular

τῷ τέκνῳ _____   to or for the child   dative singular

τοῦ ἱεροῦ _____   of the temple   genitive singular

τῶν ἔργων _____   of the works   genitive plural

τὰ δηνάρια _____   the denarii/coins   nom. or acc. plural

c. Additional notes

The ending of a noun is a clue to, but not an absolute determiner of, gender, number, and case. For example, a noun ending in -ov might be masculine accusative singular (ἄνθρωπον) or neuter nominative/accusative singular (ἔργον). A noun ending in -α might be neuter nominative/accusative plural (ἔργα) or feminine nominative singular (βασιλεία).

If the noun is accompanied by the article, however, the latter *will* determine gender, number, and case--except for the nominative vs. the accusative of neuters. For the previous examples we would find τὸν ἄνθρωπον, but τὸ ἔργον, τὰ ἔργα but ἡ βασιλεία.

EXERCISE 7-2: Translate from the Greek. Answers are grouped at the end.

1. οἱ ἀδελφοὶ διδάσκουσι τὰ τέκνα. _____

2. τὸ τέκνον ἔχει τὰ δῶρα. _____

3. τὰ τέκνα βλέπουσιν τὸ ἱερόν. _____

4. τὸ τέκνον βλέπει τὸν ἵππον. _____

5. τὸ τέκνον βλέπει ὁ ἵππος. _____

1. The brothers teach the children.
2. The child has the gifts.
3. The children see the temple.
4. The child sees the horse.
5. The horse sees the child.

LESSON 8 _____

Nouns: Use of the genitive case to indicate possession

a. Preliminary notes

One of the basic uses of the genitive case is to show possession or belonging.

- Examples: ἡ βασιλεία τοῦ θεοῦ   the kingdom of [the] God
  οἱ υἱοὶ τῆς βασιλείας   the sons of the kingdom
  ἀρχὴ τοῦ εὐαγγελίου   [the] beginning of the gospel

(In this last example English says 'the' beginning where Greek does not use the article.)

Note that there is no separate Greek word for the English word 'of'. Within these contexts the concept of possession is inherent in the genitive ending. 'Of' must be added in translation.

There are other uses of the genitive case which will be covered in later lessons, both in this and subsequent volumes of the *Workbook* series.

* * *

b. Additional vocabulary

καί	and, also
ἀλλά	but, yet
ὁ Ἰησοῦς	Jesus
ὁ ἀπόστολος	the apostle
ὁ Χριστός	the Christ
ὁ δοῦλος	the servant/slave
τὸ βιβλίον	the book
ὁ ἄγγελος	angel, messenger
λαμβάνω	I take, I receive

EXERCISE 8-1: Translate from the Greek. Answers are grouped at the end.

1. τὸ εὐαγγέλιον τοῦ θεοῦ _____

2. ὁ υἱὸς τοῦ θεοῦ _____

3. ὁ υἱὸς τοῦ ἀνθρώπου _____

4. ἡ ἀγάπη τοῦ Χριστοῦ _____

5. ἄγγελος Κυρίου _____

6. ἡ ἡμέρα Κυρίου _____

7. κεφαλὴ τῆς ἐκκλησίας _____

1. the gospel of [the] God
2. the son of [the] God
3. the son of [the] man
4. the love of Christ
5. an angel of [the] Lord
6. the day of [the] Lord
7. head of the church

c. Additional notes

In the exercise above it might be noted that--taken by itself--the phrase 'the love of Christ' is ambiguous. Does it refer to the love that Christ has for someone? Or the love that someone has for Christ?

The ambiguity exists in Greek as well as English, and the ultimate meaning must depend on elements of context.

* * *

EXERCISE 8-2: Translate from the Greek. Answers are grouped at the end.

1. οἱ λόγοι τοῦ θεοῦ _____

2. οἱ ἄνθρωποι γράφουσι τοὺς λόγους τοῦ θεοῦ

_____

3. τὰ δῶρα τῶν ἀδελφῶν _____

4. οἱ ἀπόστολοι λαμβάνουσιν τὰ δῶρα τῶν ἀδελφῶν

_____

5. ὁ Ἰησοῦς βλέπει τοὺς ἀποστόλους καὶ τὰ τέκνα

_____

1. the words of [the] God
2. the people write the words of [the] God
3. the gifts of the brothers
4. the apostles receive the gifts of the brothers
5. [the] Jesus sees the apostles and the children

LESSON 9 _____

a. Preliminary notes

The 'to be' verb in Greek is irregular and its forms must be memorized separately.

Remember that Greek verb forms include an implied subject, i.e., εἰμί can express the concept 'I am' without 'I' (ἐγώ) being added.

The verb εἰμί is called a *linking* verb; that is, it links its subject with something else. For example, in English we might say

The woman	is	a doctor.
The ball	is	red.
Their first child	was	a boy.

The second item (a doctor, red, a boy) restates or additionally defines the first (the woman, the ball, their first child) and is called the predicate nominative. In Greek, in the sentences above, both the subject and the predicate nominative would be in the nominative case.

- Examples: ὁ   ἀπόστολός ἐστιν ἀδελφός
             the   apostle   is   a brother

    εἰμὶ   δοῦλος
    I am   a slave

    καὶ   ὁ   θεός ἦν   ὁ   λόγος
    and [the] God was the word
    and the word was God   John 1:1

b. Morphology of the verb εἰμί, 'I am'

εν αρχή
ην
ο λόγος

Table 9-1: Present tense of the verb εἰμί

εἰμί	I am	ἐσμέν	we are
εἶ	you are (sing.)	ἐστέ	you are (pl.)
ἐστί(ν)	he/she/it is	εἰσί(ν)	they are

EXERCISE 9-1: Translate from the Greek

ἐστὲ ἀπόστολοι _____ you (plural) are apostles

εἰμὶ τέκνον _____ I am a child

ἐσμὲν οἱ ἄνθρωποι _____ we are the people

ἐστὶν ὁ Χριστός _____ he is the Christ

εἶ Πέτρος _____ you are Peter

ἄγγελοί εἰσιν _____ angels they are (they are angels)

τοῦ κυρίου ἐσμέν _____ of the Lord we are
(we are the Lord's)

ἀδελφοί ἐστε _____ brothers you are
(you are brothers)

EXERCISE 9-2: Translate from the Greek. Answers are grouped at the end.

1. ἐσμὲν τέκνα θεοῦ _____

2. ὁ θεὸς ἀγάπη ἐστίν_____

3. ὁ Χριστός ἐστιν κεφαλὴ τῆς ἐκκλησίας

_____

4. ἐπαγγελίας τέκνα ἐστέ _____

5. Ἰησοῦς ἐστιν ὁ Χριστός _____

6. εἰμὶ ἡ ἀλήθεια καὶ ἡ ζωή _____

7. κύριός ἐστιν ὁ υἱὸς τοῦ ἀνθρώπου

_____

1. we are children of God
2. [the] God love is   (God is love)
3. [the] Christ is head of the church
4. of promise children you are (you are children of promise)
5. Jesus is the Christ
6. I am the truth and the life
7. Lord is the son of [the] man   (the son of man is Lord)

* * *

c. Additional notes

<u>Accents:</u> All forms of εἰμί except the second person singular (εἶ) are *enclitic*, which means that the way in which they are accented, or not accented, depends on the previous word. At this point, for the purposes of this workbook, the differences need only be noted as they occur.

The second person singular (εἶ) has smooth breathing and a circumflex accent. Do not confuse this word with εἰ, which also has smooth breathing, but no accent, and means 'if'.

Although εἶ means 'you are', not 'are' alone, in the New Testament this form is often found in combination with the personal pronoun σύ -- 'you'.

- Examples: σὺ εἶ ὁ υἱὸς τοῦ θεοῦ   you are the son of [the] God
                                                                                  John 1: 49

                    σὺ εἶ ὁ χριστός   you are the Christ
                                                                                  John 11: 27

LESSON 10 _____

Masculine nouns of the first declension

a. Preliminary notes

Most nouns of the first declension are feminine but a fair number are masculine, including some quite common words (e.g., ὁ μαθητής, the disciple).

Masculine nouns of the first declension end in -ης or -ας in the nominative singular, with the largest group ending in -ης. They tend to be proper names, or to refer to a person involved in a particular occupation or activity.

- Examples: ὁ Ἀνδρέας   Andrew
             ὁ τελώνης   tax collector
             ὁ ψεύστης   liar

* * *

b. Morphology of masculine first declension nouns ending in -ης

 εν αρχή
ην
ο λόγος

Table 10-1: Declension of προφήτης ('prophet'),
a first declension masculine noun ending in -ης

	singular	plural
nom.	ὁ προφήτης	οἱ προφῆται
gen.	τοῦ προφήτου	τῶν προφητῶν
dat.	τῷ προφήτῃ	τοῖς προφήταις
acc.	τὸν προφήτην	τοὺς προφήτας

Additional masculine words of the first declension that are declined like προφήτης include:

ὁ μαθητής	the disciple	
ὁ βαπτιστής	the baptizer	
ὁ στρατιώτης	the soldier	
ὁ ὑπηρέτης	the servant, assistant	
ὁ ἑκατοντάρχης	the centurion	
ὁ ἐργάτης	the worker	
ὁ δεσπότης	the master, owner	

εν αρχή
ην
ο λόγος

Accents: Accent placement varies and should be noted; we find προφήτης and προφήτου, for example, but μαθητής and μαθητοῦ.

* * *

EXERCISE 10-1: Translate from the Greek and identify gender, number, and case.

τοὺς ἐργάτας _____   the workers; masculine plural acc.

τὰς γραφάς _____   the writings; feminine plural acc.

τοῖς μαθηταῖς _____   to or for the disciples;
                                                                                         masculine plural dative

τὸ τέκνον_____   the child; neuter singular nom./acc.

τῷ ἑκαντοτάρχῃ _____   to or for the centurion;
                                                                                          masculine singular dative

ἡ βασιλεία _____   the kingdom; feminine sing. nom.

τῶν προφητῶν _____ of the prophets; masc. plural gen.

τὸν μαθητήν _____ the disciple; masc. singular acc.

ὁ στρατιώτης _____ the soldier; masc. singular nom.

EXERCISE 10-2: Translate from the Greek. Answers are grouped at the end.

1. ὁ Ἰησοῦς λέγει τοῖς μαθηταῖς _____

2. ἐστὶν ἡ βασιλεία τῶν οὐρανῶν _____

3. ὁ νόμος καὶ οἱ προφῆται _____

4. ὁ Πέτρος βλέπει τὸν μαθητήν _____

5. στρατιώτης Χριστοῦ Ἰησοῦ _____

1. [the] Jesus says to the disciples
2. is the kingdom of the heavens
3. the law and the prophets
4. [the] Peter sees the disciple
5. a soldier of Christ Jesus

* * * *

From this point on most phrases for translation (as in Exercise 10-2) will be taken from
the New Testament with little or no adaptation. They will not necessarily be familiar out

of context, however. For example, 'is the kingdom of the heavens', above, was taken from Matthew 13: 45, and is part of a longer sentence which reads 'the kingdom of heaven is like . . . ', with the word order changed in translation.

c. Additional notes

As mentioned at the beginning of the lesson, there are other patterns of declension for first declension masculine nouns. The primary variant occurs with nouns ending in -ας, which are (1) almost exclusively proper names and therefore, (2) have only singular forms.

Here are two examples, which differ in their genitive endings:

ὁ Ἠλίας (Elijah, Elias) ὁ Βαρναβᾶς (Barnabas)
τοῦ Ἠλίου τοῦ Βαρναβᾶ
τῷ Ἠλίᾳ τῷ Βαρναβᾷ
τὸν Ἠλίαν τὸν Βαρναβᾶν

Since proper names are capitalized, and often sound similar in English (e.g., ὁ Ἀγρίππας, ὁ Κλεοπᾶς, ὁ Σατανᾶς), they can be recognized as names by the reader, and usually do not present significant problems in understanding.

It should also be noted that proper names are found in all three koine declensions.

- Examples from the second declension: ὁ Παῦλος (Paul), ὁ Πέτρος (Peter), ὁ Μᾶρκος (Mark)

- Examples from the first declension: ἡ Μαρία (Mary), ὁ Ἰωάννης (John), ὁ Ἡρῴδης (Herod), ὁ Λουκᾶς (Luke)

- Examples from the third declension (not covered as yet): ἡ Ἄρτεμις (Artemis), ὁ Σολομῶν (Solomon)

LESSON 11 _____

The declension of Ἰησοῦς, one use of αὐτός, punctuation marks

This lesson has a different arrangement from those previous, as it covers several shorter and unrelated matters.

a. The declension of Ἰησοῦς

The name Ἰησοῦς (Jesus) is, of course, one of the most common words in the New Testament. The declension is somewhat irregular, and the forms are best simply memorized.

εν αρχή
ην
ο λόγος

Table 11-1: The declension
of the name Ἰησοῦς

ὁ Ἰησοῦς
τοῦ Ἰησοῦ
τῷ Ἰησοῦ
τὸν Ἰησοῦν

Note that the genitive and dative noun forms are identical in spelling. The best translation must be determined by context and/or by the presence of the article.

* * *

b. One use of the word αὐτός

The use of αὐτός, αὐτή, αὐτό is one of the more confusing matters in koine Greek. Depending on placement and context it can function as a third person personal pronoun ('he', 'she', 'it', 'they'), as an adjective meaning 'same', or as an intensifying pronoun meaning '--self' (myself, yourself, himself, herself, etc.).

Here we will confine ourselves to one particular and common use; as a pronoun in the genitive case, indicating possession or belonging. The genitive case is αὐτοῦ in the masculine singular and αὐτῆς in the feminine singular.

- Examples: οἱ μαθηταὶ αὐτοῦ   the disciples of him (his disciples)

  ὁ ἀδελφὸς αὐτοῦ   the brother of him (his brother)

  ἡ βασιλεία αὐτοῦ   the kingdom of him (his kingdom)

  τὰ τέκνα αὐτῆς   the children of her (her children)

The English pattern puts the word 'his' (or 'her', or 'my', etc.) before the item possessed or belonging, and does not include the definite article: his book, her hand, my church.

Greek idiom places the genitive of αὐτός after the item possessed. This item is usually accompanied by the article; i.e., the phrase ὁ ἀδελφὸς αὐτοῦ does not refer to just any brother, it refers to *his* brother.

In these kinds of phrases--which are very common in the New Testament--αὐτοῦ can be translated as 'his', and αὐτῆς as 'her', and the word order changed.

The masculine genitive form αὐτοῦ is derived from the nominative form αὐτός, declined according to the rules of the second declension. The feminine genitive form αὐτῆς is derived from the nominative form αὐτή, declined according to the rules of the first declension. For the full declension of αὐτός, see Appendix 3.

* * *

EXERCISE 11-1: Translate from the Greek.

τὸν υἱὸν αὐτῆς _____ her son

τοὺς ἀδελφοὺς αὐτοῦ _____ his brothers

τῶν μαθητῶν αὐτοῦ _____ of his disciples

τοὺς δούλους αὐτοῦ _____ his servants/slaves

τῆς οἰκίας αὐτοῦ _____ of his house

αἱ ἐντολαὶ αὐτοῦ _____ his commandments

τὰ ἔργα αὐτῆς _____ her works

EXERCISE 11-2: Translate from the Greek. Answers are grouped at the end. Phrases are from the New Testament, and may be slightly adapted.

> εν αρχη
> ην
> ο λόγος

Additional vocabulary for this exercise, and vocabulary notes:

ἐν	in, on, by, with	ἐν is a preposition, and is followed by a noun or pronoun in the dative case, in the context of a prepositional phrase
ἡ φωνή	the voice	
ὁ λαός	the people	
ἀποστέλλω	I send, send out	note relationship of this verb to ὁ ἀπόστολος

κρίνω	I judge, determine	
εἶπεν	he/she said	3rd person singular aorist (past tense) of λέγω; a very common form to be memorized
ἀκούω	I hear	the person (or voice) being heard is often placed in the genitive, e.g., ἀκούω τῆς φωνῆς αὐτοῦ - I hear his voice

1. ἐν τῇ καρδίᾳ αὐτῆς _____

2. ἐν τῇ καρδίᾳ αὐτοῦ _____

3. καὶ ἡ ζωὴ ἐν τῷ υἱῷ αὐτοῦ ἐστίν _____

4. τὸν θρόνον αὐτοῦ καὶ ἐξουσίαν _____

5. καὶ Ἰωάννην τὸν ἀδελφὸν αὐτοῦ _____

6. ἐν τῷ υἱῷ αὐτοῦ Ἰησοῦ Χριστῷ _____

7. κρίνει ὁ κύριος τὸν λαὸν αὐτοῦ _____

8. εἶπεν τοῖς μαθηταῖς αὐτοῦ _____

9. ἀποστέλλει ὁ υἱὸς τοῦ ἀνθρώπου τοὺς ἀγγέλους αὐτοῦ

_____

1. in her heart   Luke 2: 51
2. in his heart   Matthew 5: 28
3. and the life in the son of him is (and life is in his son)   1 John 5: 11
4. his throne and authority   Rev 13: 2
5. and John his brother   Matthew 4: 21
6. in his son Jesus Christ   1 John 5: 20
7. judges the Lord the people of him (the Lord judges his people)   Hebrews 10: 30
8. he said to his disciples   Matthew 26: 1
9. sends the son of the man the angels of him

           (the son of man sends his angels)   Matthew 13: 41

c. Punctuation marks

Punctuation marks were not used in the oldest New Testament manuscripts we have available. In modern printed texts punctuation marks have been added to the Greek to assist the reader. The conventions are as follows:

1. The period and comma are used as the period and comma are used in English.

2. A dot above the line (e.g. ἄνθρωπος·) is used as English uses a semi-colon.

All of the above are seen in the following passage:

γράφω ὑμῖν, πατέρες,
I write to you, fathers,

ὅτι ἐγνώκατε τὸν ἀπ᾽ ἀρχῆς·
because you have known him who is from the beginning;

γράφω ὑμῖν, νεανίσκοι,
I write to you, young men,

ὅτι νενικήκατε τὸν πονηρόν.
because you have overcome the evil one.   1 John 2: 13

3. A semi-colon is used for the English question mark.

  Τί οὖν ποιήσωμεν;
  What then shall we do?   Luke 3: 10

  Ὁ προφήτης εἶ σύ;
  The prophet you are you?
  Are you the prophet?   John 1: 21

  ὁ   κηρύσσων μὴ κλέπτειν κλέπτεις;
  You who preach against stealing, do you steal?   Romans 2: 21

The question mark--because it looks like the semi-colon in English--can cause confusion.

Note that questions can be formed in different ways. English uses word order or an additional word such as 'does':

    You can see them.
    Can you see them?

    The disciple sees Jesus.
    Does the disciple see Jesus?

The added word, or change in word order, is usually obligatory in English when forming a question. It is not obligatory in Greek:

    ὁ μαθητὴς βλέπει τὸν Ἰησοῦν. The disciple sees Jesus.
    ὁ μαθητὴς βλέπει τὸν Ἰησοῦν; Does the disciple see Jesus?

In the earlier example, κλέπτεις could mean 'you steal' instead of 'do you steal?' if written without the question mark.

* * *

LESSON 12 _____

Prepositions and the prepositional phrase

a. Preliminary notes

The prepositional phrase is common both in Greek and English. The basic pattern is a preposition (e.g., 'in', 'on', 'after') followed by a noun, a pronoun, or a phrase, such as:

> The box is <u>in the cupboard</u>.
> The cake <u>on that table</u> is the best.
> She made her decision <u>after hearing from the committee</u>.

Prepositions can be thought of as answering implied questions such as 'which one?', 'when/where?', or 'how?'

> Where is the box?   Which cake is the best?   When did she make her decision?

The usual construction and meaning of a prepositional phrase is reasonably similar in koine Greek and English, and in both languages the meaning associated with a given preposition may vary (e.g., **on** the table, **on** the north side, **on** cue, short **on** cash).

But in addition, Greek prepositions are each associated with a particular declensional case, or cases. For example, the preposition ἐν, with the basic meaning of 'in', is associated with the dative case.

- Examples: ἐν τῇ οἰκίᾳ   in the house
            ἐν τοῖς οὐρανοῖς   in the heavens
            ἐν τῇ βασιλείᾳ   in the kingdom

Other prepositions may be associated with more than one case. The preposition 'ἐπί', for example, with a basic sense of 'on', 'over', but with many associated meanings, can be followed by a noun or pronoun in either the genitive or the dative or the accusative case.

- Examples:

ἐπὶ τῆς γῆς   on the earth, preposition followed by
                                  γῆ in the genitive case

ἐπὶ θρόνου αὐτοῦ   on his throne, + genitive
ἐπὶ τὴν γῆν   to the ground, into the land, + accusative
πέποιθεν ἐπὶ τὸν θεόν   trusted in [the] God, + accusative
ἠγαλλίασεν ἐπὶ τῷ θεῷ   rejoiced in [the] God, + dative
οὐκ ἐπ' ἄρτῳ μόνῳ (ἐπ' = ἐπί) not by bread alone, + dative

* * *

Several prepositions have alternative forms, depending on the letter immediately following. So, for example, μετά becomes μετ' when followed by a vowel with smooth breathing, and μεθ' when followed by a vowel with rough breathing.

μετὰ τῶν υἱῶν αὐτῆς   with her sons ('with the sons of her')
μετ' αὐτῆς   with her
μεθ' ὑμῶν   with you (plural)

<u>Accents</u>: Three prepositions (ἐν, εἰς, ἐκ) are *proclitic*, i.e., they are considered to associate so closely with the following word that they have no accent of their own.

b. The most common prepositions of koine Greek

Table 12-1, below, lists the most common prepositions found in the New Testament, together with their alternative forms, basic meaning/s, and associated declensional case/s.

The meanings listed must be thought of only as a rough guide. For prepositions taking more than one case, each case gets its own line.

Table 12-1: Common prepositions of koine Greek

Preposition and alternate forms		Meaning	Associated case
ἀπό	ἀπ', ἀφ'	from, away from	genitive
διά	δι'	through, during	genitive
		because of	accusative
εἰς		into	accusative
ἐκ	ἐξ	from, out of	genitive
ἐν		in	dative
ἐπί	ἐπ', ἐφ'	on, at the time of	genitive
		at, on the basis of	dative
		to, against	accusative
κατά	κατ', καθ'	down from, against	genitive
		according to, during	accusative
μετά	μετ', μεθ'	with	genitive
		after	accusative
παρά	παρ'	from	genitive
		beside, in the presence of	dative
		at, alongside	accusative
περί		about, concerning	genitive
		around	accusative
πρό		before	genitive
πρός		to	accusative
σύν		with	dative
ὑπέρ		on behalf of	genitive
		over, above	accusative
ὑπό	ὑπ', ὑφ'	by	genitive
		under, below	accusative

For future reference, do not confuse the preposition εἰς with the masculine nominative form of the number one, εἷς, or the preposition ἐν with the neuter nominative/accusative form of the number one, ἕν. In addition, the preposition ἐκ has an alternative form ἐξ, used before vowels; do not confuse this form with ἕξ, the number six.

* * *

There is an important point about cases to be made here; the oblique cases (genitive, dative, accusative) are used in prepositional phrases, yes, but--as we saw earlier--they are also used on their own.

So, for example, in the prepositional phrase μετὰ τῶν υἱῶν αὐτῆς ('with her sons'), the word for *sons* is in the genitive case because it is part of a prepositional phrase starting with μετά, and μετά meaning 'with' is followed by the genitive.

But in the phrase ἡ μήτηρ τῶν υἱῶν Ζεβεδαίου ('the mother of the sons of Zebedee') there is no preposition. The word for *sons* is in the genitive because these sons belong to this mother, and an extra word--in this case, 'of'--must be added in translation to make the relationship clear.

EXERCISE 12-1: Translate from the Greek.

> εν αρχή
> ην
> ο λόγος

ἐν ἡμέραις Ἡρῴδου _____ in [the] days of Herod

ἐν τῇ οἰκίᾳ _____ in the house

ἀπὸ τῶν ἔργων αὐτῆς _____ from the works of her
(from her works)

ἀπ' αὐτοῦ _____ from him

ἀπὸ τῶν καρδιῶν _____ from the hearts

εἰς τὴν βασιλείαν _____ into the kingdom

εἰς τὴν οἰκίαν _____ into the house

ἐκ τῶν οὐρανῶν _____ from the heavens

ἐκ τῆς καρδίας _____ out of the heart

ἐξ οἰκίας εἰς οἰκίαν _____ out of a house into a house ('from house to house')

ἐκ τοῦ ἱεροῦ _____ out of the temple

μετὰ Μαρίας _____ with Mary

μετὰ τῶν ἀγγέλων _____ with the angels

c. Additional notes

The preposition μετά, used with the basic meaning of 'after', and accompanied by the accusative, is used very commonly to designate the passage of time in a narrative. Μετά is also often found in combination with the demonstrative pronouns 'τοῦτο', meaning 'this', or 'ταῦτα', meaning 'these', as in 'these things' (happened).

- Examples:

καὶ	μετὰ	ἡμέρας	ἓξ	Mark 9: 2
and	after	days	six	

and after six days

Μετὰ	τοῦτο	κατέβη	εἰς	Καφαρναοὺμ	John 2: 12
After	this	he went down	to	Capernaum	

Μετὰ	ταῦτα	ἀπῆλθεν	ὁ	Ἰησοῦς	John 6: 1
After	these	went away	[the]	Jesus	

After this Jesus went away

* * *

The preposition κατά has two meanings that seem very different. With the genitive case it can mean 'against', as in:

ὁ	ἀδελφός	σου	ἔχει	τι	κατὰ σοῦ	Matthew 5: 23
the	brother	of you	has	something	against you	

your brother has something against you

But κατά can also mean 'according to', with the accusative, and is the preposition seen at the beginning of the gospels:

Κατὰ Μαθθαῖον	According to Matthew
Κατὰ Μᾶρκον	According to Mark
Κατὰ Λουκᾶν	According to Luke
Κατὰ Ἰωάννην	According to John

Κατά is also used in the idiom κατ' ἰδίαν, which is fairly frequent, meaning 'by themselves', or 'by himself', or 'privately'.

Τότε	προσελθόντες	οἱ μαθηταὶ	τῷ Ἰησοῦ	κατ' ἰδίαν	Matthew 17: 19
Then	came	the disciples	to [the] Jesus	privately	

Then the disciples came to Jesus privately

LESSON 13 _____

Introduction to the Greek adjective

a. Preliminary notes

In English, adjectives do not change form. A faithful child, a faithful man, and faithful women all employ the same--and only--form of the adjective 'faithful'.

Greek adjectives agree with the noun they modify in gender, number, and case. In other words, they change their form (spelling) according to their associated noun.

- Examples:

    ὁ **πιστὸς** δοῦλος   the **faithful** servant = masculine nominative singular

    πιστοῖς ἀνθρώποις   to/for **faithful** people = masculine dative plural

    οἱ λόγοι **πιστοί**   the words **faithful** (the trustworthy words) =
                                                    masculine nominative plural

We have learned that nouns have a possible ten forms, but adjectives can modify a word of any gender and must therefore have more. In theory an adjective could have thirty forms, ten each for masculine, feminine, and neuter; in reality there are never so many. Accusative neuter forms are always identical to nominative neuter forms, for one thing; in addition, the vocative form is often identical to the nominative.

Notice, in the examples given above, that the ending of the adjective πιστός is the same in all cases (barring accents) as the ending of the noun it modifies:

πιστὸς δοῦλος, πιστοῖς ἀνθρώποις, λόγοι πιστοί

This is sometimes true, but by no means always. Therefore, knowing a noun's form may help with an adjective's form--but not in every case, as will be seen.

* * *

We will start with adjectives of the 'second/first' declension, which means that the masculine and neuter forms are declined like nouns of the second declension, and the feminine forms like nouns of the first declension. Review Tables 3-2, 4-1, and 4-2.

* * *

b. Morphology of two adjectives of the second/first declension

In tables showing the declension of adjectives, masculine forms will be located on the left, then feminine, then neuter. Plural forms will be placed underneath the singular forms.

Table 13-1: Declension of the adjective μικρός, small

nom.	μικρός	μικρά	μικρόν
gen.	μικροῦ	μικρᾶς	μικροῦ
dat.	μικρῷ	μικρᾷ	μικρῷ
acc.	μικρόν	μικράν	μικρόν
nom.	μικροί	μικραί	μικρά
gen.	μικρῶν	μικρῶν	μικρῶν
dat.	μικροῖς	μικραῖς	μικροῖς
acc.	μικρούς	μικράς	μικρά

The feminine forms of this adjective follow first declension nouns ending in -α (see Table 4-1).

Table 13-2: Declension of the adjective πιστός, faithful

nom.	πιστός	πιστή	πιστόν
gen.	πιστοῦ	πιστῆς	πιστοῦ
dat.	πιστῷ	πιστῇ	πιστῷ
acc.	πιστόν	πιστήν	πιστόν
nom.	πιστοί	πισταί	πιστά
gen.	πιστῶν	πιστῶν	πιστῶν
dat.	πιστοῖς	πισταῖς	πιστοῖς
acc.	πιστούς	πιστάς	πιστά

The feminine forms of this adjective follow first declension nouns ending in -η (see Table 4-2).

In a dictionary, adjectives are often listed with abbreviated endings for the genders; i.e., μικρός may be listed as μικρός, -ά, όν, meaning μικρός, μικρά, μικρόν.

* * *

Other adjectives of similar type include:

εν αρχή ην ο λόγος

ἀγαθός, ἀγαθή, ἀγαθόν	good, useful
ἅγιος, ἁγία, ἅγιον	sacred, holy
ἀγαπητός, ἀγαπητή, ἀγαπητόν	beloved
δίκαιος, δικαία, δίκαιον	righteous, just
πρῶτος, πρώτη, πρῶτον	foremost, first
πονηρός, πονηρά, πονηρόν	wicked, bad
καλός, καλή, καλόν	good, honest

* * *

<u>Accents</u>: The reader may have noticed that the accent on the adjectives μικρός and πιστός remains on the final syllable for all forms; this will be a general rule for those adjectives with an accent on the final syllable of the masculine nominative singular. Other adjectives, however have their accent on a different syllable, and it may move: ἅγιος becomes ἁγία in the feminine nominative singular, for example.

The rules of accent present so many complications that it seems counterproductive to focus on them at the start. I suggest careful attention to accents while reading text, but less worry when trying to produce Greek words on your own.

* * *

EXERCISE 13-1: Translate from the Greek.

ὁ ἀγαθὸς ἄνθρωπος _____ the good person

ὁ πονηρὸς ἄνθρωπος _____ the bad person

ἐγὼ ἀγαθός εἰμι _____ I good I am (I am good)

Ἰησοῦν Χριστὸν δίκαιον _____ Jesus Christ [the] righteous

ἡ ἐντολὴ ἁγία _____ the commandment [is] holy

ἐντολὴ πρώτη _____ commandment first/foremost

τὰ πρῶτα ἔργα _____ the first works

ἅγίαι γραφαί _____ holy writings

τοῦ ἀγαπητοῦ ἀδελφοῦ _____ of the beloved brother

c. Additional notes

Adjectives often function as substantives; that is, they act as a noun, or (perhaps more correctly) imply the existence of an associated noun. So 'the just person' could be expressed as ὁ δίκαιος ἄνθρωπος or simply ὁ δίκαιος.

- Example: ὁ ἅγιος   τοῦ θεοῦ   Mark 1: 24
  the holy [one]   of God

- Example: βρέχει ἐπὶ δικαίους   καὶ   ἀδίκους   Matthew 5: 45
  it rains on just [people]   and   unjust [people]

EXERCISE 13-2: Translate from the Greek.
Answers are grouped at the end.

> εν αρχή
> ην
> ο λόγος

Additional vocabulary for this exercise, and vocabulary notes:

ἔσχατος, -η, -ον	last, final	
ὁ Ἀδάμ	Adam	an indeclinable noun; that is all its forms are spelled in the same way
ἐκβάλλω	drive out, bring forth	

ἦν	he/she/it was	a past tense form of εἰμί; a very common form to be memorized

1. ἄνθρωπος ἀγαθὸς καὶ δίκαιος _____

2. ἐν καρδίᾳ καλῇ καὶ ἀγαθῇ _____

3. ὁ πρῶτος ἄνθρωπος Ἀδάμ _____

4. εἶ ὁ ἅγιος τοῦ θεοῦ _____

5. τέκνον ἀγαπητὸν καὶ πιστὸν ἐν κυρίῳ _____

6. τὰ ἔργα αὐτοῦ πονηρὰ ἦν, τὰ ἔργα τοῦ ἀδελφοῦ αὐτοῦ δίκαια

_____

7. ὁ ἀγαθὸς ἄνθρωπος ἐκ τοῦ ἀγαθοῦ θησαυροῦ ἐκβάλλει ἀγαθά

_____

8. καὶ ὁ πονηρὸς ἄνθρωπος ἐκ τοῦ πονηροῦ θησαυροῦ ἐκβάλλει πονηρά

_____

9. ἐγώ εἰμι ὁ πρῶτος καὶ ὁ ἔσχατος _____

10. πιστοῖς ἐν Χριστῷ Ἰησοῦ _____

1. a person good and righteous   Luke 23: 50

2. in heart honest and good (honest and good in heart)   Luke 8: 15

3. the first man, Adam   1 Cor. 15: 45

4. you are the holy one of [the] God   Mark 1 :24

5. a child beloved and faithful in [the] Lord   1 Cor. 4: 17

6. his works were[1] wicked, the works of his brother [were] righteous 1 John 3: 12

7. the good man from the good treasure brings forth good [things]   Matt. 12: 35

8. and the wicked man from the wicked treasure

                    brings forth wicked [things]   Matt. 12: 35

9. I am the first and the last   Rev. 1: 17

10. to/for the faithful in Christ Jesus   Ephesians 1: 1

---

[1] Koine neuter plural nouns sometimes take a verb in the singular, in this case ἦν. So here ἦν must be translated (they) 'were' instead of 'was'.

LESSON 14

Adjectives, continued: attributive and predicative adjectives

a. Preliminary notes

As we advance in the koine beyond isolated words and short phrases it is inevitable that complications arise. Each language has its own patterns and idiom, and a one-to-one correspondence between words becomes the exception.

One of these complications involves the attributive vs. the predicate use of adjectives. Compare these two sentences in English:

> The ball is red.
> The red ball rolled down the hill.

In both cases, 'red' is an adjective. In the first sentence, it states something about the ball, i.e., it is red. This sentence could be in answer to the question, "What color is the ball?" In the second sentence 'red' identifies the ball in question, the one that rolled down the hill. It might be in answer to the question, "Which ball rolled down the hill?"

The first sentence is an example of 'red' as a predicate adjective. The second sentence is an example of 'red' used as an attributive adjective.

We interpret these sentences correctly and naturally in English, where an attributive adjective usually comes before its noun, and a predicate adjective follows a linking verb, and there's the end to it. But in Greek the distinction is key and the rules of word order are more complicated. The discussion that follows will give an overview; keep in mind the possibility of exception and nuance.

1. When a noun is accompanied by the article the choice between attributive and predicate is generally clear.

    a. If the adjective is immediately preceded by the article, it is attributive. The most common order is either:

article-adjective-noun, e.g., τὰ καλὰ ἔργα, 'the good works'

or

article-noun-article-adjective, e.g., τὰ ἔργα τὰ καλά, 'the good works'.

b. If the adjective is not preceded by the article, the adjective is predicative. The most common order is either:

article-noun-adjective, e.g., τὰ ἔργα καλά, 'the works are good'

or

adjective-article-noun, e.g., καλὰ τὰ ἔργα, 'the works are good'.

2. When a noun is *not* accompanied by the article the choice is less clear. Ἀγαθὸς ἄνθρωπος might mean 'a good man' or 'a man is good'. Context must be considered in translating.

* * *

Notice that in situation 1 (b) above, a linking verb must be added to the translation. In English, linking verbs are usually obligatory; 'Andrew is an apostle' could be a complete sentence, but 'Andrew an apostle' is not.

In Greek the linking verb may be omitted.

- Examples: ὁ μὲν νόμος ἅγιος   Romans 7: 12
  the then law   holy
  so then, the law [is] holy

  αὐτῶν πονηρὰ τὰ ἔργα   John 3: 19
  of them evil   the works
  their works [were] evil

b. Summary of the patterns of use for substantive, attributive, and predicate adjectives

<u>Substantive adjective</u>
An adjective without associated noun or pronoun
ὁ δίκαιος - the righteous person

article-adjective

<u>Attributive adjective, noun with the article</u>
An adjective immediately or closely preceded by the article
ὁ δίκαιος ἄνθρωπος - the righteous person
ὁ ἄνθρωπος ὁ δίκαιος - the righteous person

article-adjective-noun
article-noun-article-adjective

<u>Predicate adjective, noun with the article</u>
The adjective is not preceded by the article.
δίκαιος ὁ ἄνθρωπος - the person is righteous
ὁ ἄνθρωπος δίκαιος - the person is righteous

adjective-article-noun
article-noun-adjective

<u>Attributive or predicate adjective, noun without the article</u>
The choice of attributive or predicate adjective
must be made on the basis of context.
δίκαιος ἄνθρωπος ⎤ both could mean 'a righteous person'
ἄνθρωπος δίκαιος ⎦ or 'a person is righteous'

adjective-noun
noun-adjective

EXERCISE 14-1: Translate from the Greek. Identify the type of adjective used.

ἡ βασιλεία ἡ καλή _____ the good kingdom
attributive

καλὴ ἡ βασιλεία_____ the kingdom is good
predicative

τῆς καλῆς βασιλείας _____ of the good kingdom
attributive

πονηρὸς ὁ ἵππος _____ the horse is wicked
predicative

τοῦ πονηροῦ ἵππου _____ of the wicked horse
attributive

τὰς ἀγαθὰς ἐπαγγελίας _____ the good promises
attributive

ἡ ἐπαγγελία ἀγαθή _____ the promise is good
predicative

τῷ ἀγαπητῷ ἀδελφῷ _____ to/for the beloved brother
attributive

ἀγαπητοὶ οἱ ἀδελφοί _____ the brothers are beloved
predicative

τὸ τέκνον τὸ πρῶτον _____ the first child
attributive

πρῶτα τὰ τέκνα _____ the children are first
predicative

EXERCISE 14-2: Translate from the Greek. Answers are grouped at the end.

ἐν ἀρχή
ην
ο λόγος

Additional vocabulary for this exercise, and vocabulary notes:

μέν   so, then   by itself, this particle can indicate continuation;
                                    other translations often possible

ἡμῶν   our, ours   the genitive plural of the personal pronoun;
                                    a very common form

οὗτοι   these (people),   a plural demonstrative pronoun
               they

τὸ ὄνομα   the name   a third declension noun, to be covered in
                                    the second volume of the *Workbook* series

ἡ γῆ   earth, land, soil

ἔσονται   they will be   the future 3rd person plural of εἰμί

1. ὁ ἀγαπητὸς ἡμῶν ἀδελφὸς Παῦλος _____

2. ἐπὶ τὴν γῆν τὴν καλὴν _____

3. ἔσονται οἱ ἔσχατοι πρῶτοι καὶ οἱ πρῶτοι ἔσχατοι

_____

4. καὶ ἡ φωνὴ ἡ πρώτη _____

5. καὶ ἅγιον τὸ ὄνομα αὐτοῦ _____

6. ὁ μὲν νόμος ἅγιος, καὶ ἡ ἐντολὴ ἁγία καὶ δικαία καὶ ἀγαθή

_____

7. ὁ πρῶτος οὐρανὸς καὶ ἡ πρώτη γῆ _____

8. ἐγώ εἰμι τὸ Ἄλφα καὶ τὸ Ὦ, λέγει Κύριος, ὁ θεός

_____

9. ἐγὼ τὸ Ἄλφα καὶ τὸ Ὦ, ὁ πρῶτος καὶ ὁ ἔσχατος

_____

10. οὗτοί εἰσιν οἱ υἱοὶ τῆς βασιλείας

_____

11. εἰσιν οἱ υἱοὶ τοῦ πονηροῦ _____

1. the beloved our brother Paul (our beloved brother Paul)   2 Peter 3: 15
2. on the soil the good (on the good soil)   Matthew 13: 8
3. they will be the last first and the first last
                        (the last will be first and the first last)   Matthew 20: 16
4. and the voice the first (and the first voice)   Rev. 4: 1
5. and holy the name of him (and holy [is] his name)   Luke 1: 49
6. so then the law [is] holy, and the commandment [is]
             holy and righteous and good   Romans 7: 12
7. the first heaven and the first earth   Rev. 21: 1
8. I am the Alpha and the Omega, says [the] Lord, [the] God   Rev. 1: 8
9. I [am] the Alpha and the Omega, the first and the last   Rev. 22: 13
10. these/they are the sons of the kingdom   Matthew 13: 38
11. they are the sons of the evil [one]   Matthew 13: 38

* * *

c. Additional notes

Other adjectives follow other patterns of declension. The adjective 'ἀληθής, ἀληθής, ἀληθές' ('true'), for example, has a set of endings very different from the endings of μικρός, πιστός, et al. Ἀληθής is considered an adjective of the third declension, and will be covered after the lesson on third declension nouns, in the next volume of this series.

LESSON 15 _____

Review exercises

EXERCISE 15-1: Conjugate the verb ἀκούω ('I hear') in the present tense:

_____	_____	ἀκούω	ἀκούομεν
_____	_____	ἀκούεις	ἀκούετε
_____	_____	ἀκούει	ἀκούουσι(ν)

EXERCISE 15-2: Translate from the Greek.

βλέπετε _____   you (pl.) see

τῆς ζωῆς _____   of the life

τοῖς ἀγγέλοις αὐτοῦ _____   to/for his angels

πίνω _____   I drink

τῆς πρώτης ἐντολῆς _____   of the first commandment

ὁ ποταμὸς ζωῆς _____   the river of life

γράφει ὁ Πέτρος _____   Peter writes

διδάσκεις τὰ τέκνα; _____ are you teaching the children?

λαμβάνει _____ he/she takes or receives

ἡ βασιλεία τοῦ θεοῦ _____ the kingdom of God

ὁ Ἰησοῦς εἶπεν _____ Jesus said

ὁ Πέτρος εἶπεν τῷ Ἰησοῦ _____ Peter said to Jesus

ὁ υἱός μου ὁ ἀγαπητός _____ my beloved son

ἀπὸ τῆς γῆς _____ from the earth/land

ἀκούομεν _____ we hear

EXERCISE 15-3: Translate (most) of the first five verses of the gospel of John. A word-for-word translation is given at the end, followed by a standard translation (English Standard Version, 2011).

εν αρχή
ην
ο λόγος

Additional vocabulary for this exercise, and vocabulary notes:

οὗτος	this (person), he	a demonstrative pronoun; the singular form of οὗτοι, seen in the previous lesson
πάντα	all (things)	all *things* in this context; the plural neuter form of the adjective πᾶς, πᾶσα, πᾶν - all, every
ἐγένετο	came into being, was made	a 3rd person sing. past tense of the verb γίνομαι; a common form

τὸ φῶς	the light	a neuter, third declension noun
ἡ σκοτία	the darkness	a first declension noun
φαίνω	appear, shine	
αὐτό	it	*it* in this context; the neuter singular form of αὐτός, used as a pronoun
οὐ κατέλαβεν	has not overcome	κατέλαβεν is a past tense form of the verb καταλαμβάνω; the word οὐ is the negating adverb ('not').

1. Ἐν ἀρχῇ ἦν ὁ λόγος _____

   καὶ ὁ λόγος ἦν πρὸς τὸν θεόν, _____

   καὶ θεὸς ἦν ὁ λόγος. _____

2. οὗτος ἦν ἐν ἀρχῇ πρὸς τὸν θεόν._____

3. πάντα δι' αὐτοῦ ἐγένετο, _____

   [part of verse 3 omitted]

4. ἐν αὐτῷ ζωὴ ἦν, _____

καὶ ἡ ζωὴ ἦν _____

τὸ φῶς τῶν ἀνθρώπων· _____

5. καὶ τὸ φῶς _____

ἐν τῇ σκοτίᾳ φαίνει, _____

καὶ ἡ σκοτία αὐτὸ οὐ κατέλαβεν. _____

John 1: 1-5

1. Ἐν ἀρχῇ ἦν ὁ λόγος — In beginning was the word
καὶ ὁ λόγος ἦν πρὸς τὸν θεόν — and the word was before the God
καὶ θεὸς ἦν ὁ λόγος. — and God was the word.

2. οὗτος ἦν ἐν ἀρχῇ πρὸς τὸν θεόν. — he was in beginning before the God.

3. πάντα δι᾽ αὐτοῦ ἐγένετο, — all things through him were made,

[. . .]

4. ἐν αὐτῷ ζωὴ ἦν, — in him life was,
καὶ ἡ ζωὴ ἦν — and the life was
τὸ φῶς τῶν ἀνθρώπων· — the light of the people;

5. καὶ τὸ φῶς — and the light

ἐν τῇ σκοτίᾳ φαίνει,   in the darkness shines,
καὶ ἡ σκοτία αὐτὸ οὐ κατέλαβεν.   and the darkness it has not overcome.

1. In the beginning was the Word, and the Word was with God, and the Word was God.
2. He was in the beginning with God.
3. All things were made through him, [omitted: and without him was not any thing made that was made.]
4. In him was life, and the life was the light of men.
5. The light shines in the darkness, and the darkness has not overcome it.

* * * * *

APPENDIX 1

A list of resources for koine Greek

Below is a short list, limited to those resources I thought most useful for beginners.

a. The Greek New Testament

The Greek New Testament with Dictionary, 4th edition
Aland, Aland, Karavidopoulos, Martini, and Metzger, editors
Deutsche Bibelgesellschaft, 2010
A 5th edition is upcoming. This is a standard ('USB4') version of the Greek New Testament used in many classes. Greek only. The paper is thin and the font somewhat italicized, but still reasonably large and readable. The inclusion of a dictionary is welcome.

The New Testament in the Original Greek: Byzantine Textform
Robinson and Pierpont, editors
Chilton Book Publishing, 2005
This volume uses the 'Byzantine Textform' version of the Greek New Testament, and the editors include a lengthy essay in support of their choice. The book itself is nicely designed, with heavy paper and an excellent font. Greek only. No dictionary.

The Greek New Testament: UBS4 With NRSV & NIV
John R. Kohlenberger III, editor
Zondervan, 1993
The standard Greek text flanked by two English translations; the New Revised Standard Version, and the New International Version. Text size is readable. No dictionary.

A Reader's Greek New Testament, 2nd edition
Goodrich and Lukaszewski, editors
Zondervan, 2007
This volume assumes a basic vocabulary on the part of the reader (to whit, every word used more than 30 times in the NT, which amounts to some 450+ words) and provides a running dictionary at the bottom of the page for each word used less often. (A dictionary at the end does give all the words used more than 30 times.)
The basic concept is good, although the print is light, which makes this particular NT somewhat less readable. On the other hand, the volume is light in weight and portable.

There are at least two other versions of a similarly arranged New Testament available, listed below. I have not seen either of these so cannot comment further.

UBS Greek New Testament: Reader's Edition with Textual Notes
Crossway, 2011

The UBS Greek New Testament: A Reader's Edition
B. Newman, editor
Hendrickson Publishers, 2007

Also note:

The New Greek-English Interlinear New Testament
J.D. Douglas, editor
Tyndale House, 1993

Less intimidating than an all-Greek New Testament, this volume has the (basic/literal) English translation printed below each line of Greek. The New Revised Standard Version is also printed at the side, so the reader can compare a word-for-word rendering of the Greek with a fluent translation. If nothing else, an interlinear NT makes the difficulties of good translation very clear.

b. Textbooks

I list below only those books I have used myself, with comments on their suitability for self-study.

New Testament Greek for Beginners, second edition
J. Gresham Machen and Dan G. McCartney
Pearson/Prentice Hall, 2004

The old standby, now in an updated edition. This is the book I return to for straightforward explanations of basic grammar; it is not, however, intended for the self-study learner. No keys to exercises.

Learn New Testament Greek: 3rd edition
John H. Dobson
Baker Academic, 2005

My personal favorite for self-study. Many exercises with keys. The approach involves translating numerous short phrases and sentences, thereby familiarizing students with some of the rhythms of the language before moving to longer passages. The weakness may be in the lack of an organized approach to grammar.

Beginning Greek: A Functional Approach
Stephen W. Pain
Oxford University Press, 1961

Old-school, for those who want to dive in head-first. This book might be useful for those with a wider interest in the Greek language: Part 1 covers a set of readings from the gospel of John, and Part 2 goes back to classical Greek, with readings from the *Anabasis* of Xenophon. Only for the confident self-studier.

Basics of Biblical Greek Grammar
William D. Mounce
Zondervan, 2003, 2009

I am familiar only with the second edition; a third edition is now available. Possibly the most widely used text in American classrooms. I cannot recommend for self-study by itself, as there are no exercises in the text. There is a separate workbook available, but without keys, although a set of answers is now available on-line.

c. Dictionaries and other helps

Over the years I made do with the dictionary included with the Greek New Testament edited by Aland et al. (see above), supplemented by the Liddell-Scott *Intermediate Greek-English Lexicon*, a dictionary more often used by students of classical Greek, but which includes the koine vocabulary. There is now a very useful dictionary associated with the 'greattreasures.org' website (see below); I recommend that you look at this first.

Two well-reviewed dictionaries available on amazon.com are:

Vine's Complete Expository Dictionary of Old and New Testament Words: With Topical Index
W. E. Vine and M. Unger
Thomas Nelson, 1996

Complete Word Study Dictionary: New Testament
S. Zodhiates
AMG Publishers, 1992

Also note:

Complete Vocabulary Guide to the Greek New Testament, revised edition
W. Trenchard
Zondervan, 1998

I have found this volume useful, especially for the principal parts of verbs. It also lists all words in the New Testament in order of frequency. Although not really a dictionary, it does provide basic meanings for all words.

* * *

d. On-line resources

Websites sometimes seem to change monthly, and it may be more convenient to find the links via the *Workbook* website, which will be updated. The site address is:

koineworkbook.wordpress.com

Below are a few particularly useful resources:

www.greattreasures.org

This is my favorite New Testament Greek website. You will need to sign in with email and password, but once signed in you can display the Greek New Testament together with several English translations of your choice. Clicking on a Greek word brings up the definition and its declension or conjugation (under 'word forms'). Verbs are also parsed.

www.biblehub.com

Also a very useful site. At the very top of the page you will have a choice of books of the Bible; choose Matthew (or any other New Testament book) and you will see a page with various English translations of a single verse.
At that point, click on 'Interlinear', 'Greek', or 'Lexicon'; you will be taken to a page with the Greek text and associated information.

www.biblicalgreek.org

If you click on 'helps', either at the top of the page or on the side menu, you will be taken to a page with links to a variety of topics, including the pronunciation of Greek.

www.teknia.com/greek-dictionary

The Teknia site has an on-line koine dictionary that is straightforward and usable.

* * *

APPENDIX 2 _____

The pronunciation of koine Greek

a. Why I use the pronunciation rules of modern Greek in reading koine

The arguments in favor of using the modern pronunciation include those below. For further discussion, see the resources listed at the end of this appendix.

1) The modern pronunciation is arguably closer to the original koine than the most common alternative (the standard, academic 'Erasmian' pronunciation).

2) The modern pronunciation is the result of a few thousand years of language evolution, resulting in a spoken word that sounds natural. The somewhat arbitrary, Erasmian rules -- in my opinion -- do not produce a natural-sounding language.

3) This pronunciation of koine can be heard *in use*, if the student wishes to visit a Greek Orthodox parish. At least some Greek Orthodox churches in the United States read New Testament passages in the original Greek during the liturgy; the modern pronunciation is used.

In addition, you can hear the New Testament read aloud with the modern pronunciation on various websites (information and links below). This is the only opportunity a student has of hearing these texts read in Greek by a native speaker of a closely associated language.

4) If a student has any interest in modern Greek, the argument for practice in its pronunciation is obvious.

It has been said that the Erasmian pronunciation is pedagogically superior, since each letter corresponds to only one sound, and each sound to only one letter. I would argue, however, that 'one letter-one sound' is less important in the case of koine Greek, where the emphasis is on written texts.

At any rate, whichever system the student picks, consistency is key. Choose the one that appeals to you, if you are on your own, or the one that will be used in class, if you are not.

b. Rules for the 'Erasmian' pronunciation of koine Greek

There are several versions of the Erasmian system, differing in a few particulars; the one presented below corresponds to the rules give in *New Testament Greek for Beginners, Second Edition*, by Machen and McCartney (Pearson/Prentice Hall, 2004); see pp. 31 ff.

Single letters

A	α	ἄλφα	ah, as in father
B	β	βῆτα	b, as in boy
Γ	γ	γάμμα	g, as in got
Δ	δ	δέλτα	d, as in dog
E	ε	ἐ ψιλόν	e, as in met
Z	ζ	ζῆτα	dz, or z as in daze
H	η	ἦτα	a, as in rate
Θ	θ	θῆτα	th, as in think
I	ι	ἰῶτα	long i, i as in machine
			short i, i as in bit
K	κ	κάππα	k, as in keep
Λ	λ	λάμβδα	l, as in let
M	μ	μῦ	m, as in man
N	ν	νῦ	n, as in never
Ξ	ξ	ξῖ	x, as in taxi

Ο	ο	ὂ μικρόν	o, as in oval
Π	π	πῖ	p, as in Peter
Ρ	ϱ	ῥῶ	r, as in room
Σ	σ,ς	σίγμα	s, as in sea
Τ	τ	ταῦ	t, as in tea
Υ	υ	ὖ ψιλόν	French u, or oo as in boot
Φ	φ	φῖ	f, as in fun
Χ	χ	χῖ	somewhat like ch as in German 'Bach'
Ψ	ψ	ψῖ	ps, as in maps
Ω	ω	ὦ μέγα	o, as in note

Double vowels

αι	ai as in aisle
ει	a as in rate (= η)
οι	oi as in oil
αυ	ou as in out
ευ	eu as in feud
ου	ou as in soup

* * *

c. Greek pronunciation: other resources

1. Books

Any textbook in modern Greek will go into detail regarding the modern pronunciation, and most koine textbooks will cover the Erasmian, but an alternative (and cheaper) approach is to look for this information on-line. See below for those resources.

The three books listed here offer general information about the pronunciation of Greek over the ages. They are detailed and scholarly, and most appropriate for readers wishing to advance beyond a beginning level in the language.

Greek: A History of the Language and its Speakers, 2nd edition
G. Horrocks
Wiley-Blackwell, 2014

The Greek Language
Leonard R. Palmer
University of Oklahoma Press, 1996

Vox Graeca: The Pronunciation of Classical Greek, 3rd edition
W. Sidney Allen
Cambridge University Press, 1987

* * *

2. On-line resources, including the Greek New Testament read aloud

All links given below will also be posted on the *Workbook* website.

a. **The Institute of Biblical Greek** has a central page for issues of koine Greek pronunciation. This is a good place to start for help with the Erasmian system.

http://www.biblicalgreek.org/links/pronunciation.php

b. The inimitable **Harry Foundalis** has a *very* thorough discussion of modern Greek pronunciation, starting here:

http://www.foundalis.com/lan/grkalpha.htm

c. Wikipedia also has a discussion of modern Greek phonology.

d. The **Bible.is** website has a version of the Greek New Testament read very fluently by a native speaker of Greek. You must sign into this website and choose Greek as the language.

www.bible.is

e. The **Let's Read Greek** website has an impressive list of audio files for the Greek New Testament. Various pronunciations are available and evaluated.

http://www.letsreadgreek.com/resources/greekntaudio.htm

* * *

Appendix 3 _____

Declension and conjugation tables

1. Declension of the article

	Singular			Plural		
	masc.	fem.	neut.	masc.	fem.	neut.
nom.	ὁ	ἡ	τό	οἱ	αἱ	τά
gen.	τοῦ	τῆς	τοῦ	τῶν	τῶν	τῶν
dat.	τῷ	τῇ	τῷ	τοῖς	ταῖς	τοῖς
acc.	τόν	τήν	τό	τούς	τάς	τά

2. Declension of καρδία, a first declension feminine noun

Singular		Plural	
nom.	καρδία	nom.	καρδίαι
gen.	καρδίας	gen.	καρδιῶν
dat.	καρδίᾳ	dat.	καρδίαις
acc.	καρδίαν	acc.	καρδίας

3. Declension of γραφή, a first declension feminine noun

Singular		Plural	
nom.	γραφή	nom.	γραφαί
gen.	γραφῆς	gen.	γραφῶν
dat.	γραφῇ	dat.	γραφαῖς
acc.	γραφήν	acc.	γραφάς

4. Declension of προφήτης, a first declension masculine noun

Singular		Plural	
nom.	προφήτης	nom.	προφῆται
gen.	προφήτου	gen.	προφητῶν
dat.	προφήτῃ	dat.	προφήταις
acc.	προφήτην	acc.	προφήτας

5. Declension of θεός, a second declension masculine noun

Singular		Plural	
nom.	θεός	nom.	θεοί
gen.	θεοῦ	gen.	θεῶν
dat.	θεῷ	dat.	θεοῖς
acc.	θεόν	acc.	θεούς

6. Declension of δῶρον, a second declension neuter noun

Singular		Plural	
nom.	δῶρον	nom.	δῶρα
gen.	δώρου	gen.	δώρων
dat.	δώρῳ	dat.	δώροις
acc.	δῶρον	acc.	δῶρα

7. The declension of the name Ἰησοῦς

nom.	Ἰησοῦς
gen.	Ἰησοῦ
dat.	Ἰησοῦ
acc.	Ἰησοῦν

8. Declension of the adjective μικρός

Singular

	masc.	fem.	neut.
nom.	μικρός	μικρά	μικρόν
gen.	μικροῦ	μικρᾶς	μικροῦ
dat.	μικρῷ	μικρᾷ	μικρῷ
acc.	μικρόν	μικράν	μικρόν

Plural

	masc.	fem.	neut.
nom.	μικροί	μικραί	μικρά
gen.	μικρῶν	μικρῶν	μικρῶν
dat.	μικροῖς	μικραῖς	μικροῖς
acc.	μικρούς	μικράς	μικρά

9. Declension of the adjective πιστός

Singular

	masc.	fem.	neut.
nom.	πιστός	πιστή	πιστόν
gen.	πιστοῦ	πιστῆς	πιστοῦ
dat.	πιστῷ	πιστῇ	πιστῷ
acc.	πιστόν	πιστήν	πιστόν

Plural

	masc.	fem.	neut.
nom.	πιστοί	πισταί	πιστά
gen.	πιστῶν	πιστῶν	πιστῶν
dat.	πιστοῖς	πισταῖς	πιστοῖς
acc.	πιστούς	πιστάς	πιστά

10. Declension of αὐτός, αὐτή, αὐτό

Singular

	masc.	fem.	neut.
nom.	αὐτός	αὐτή	αὐτό
gen.	αὐτοῦ	αὐτῆς	αὐτοῦ
dat.	αὐτῷ	αὐτῇ	αὐτῷ
acc.	αὐτόν	αὐτήν	αὐτό

Plural

	masc.	fem.	neut.
nom.	αὐτοί	αὐταί	αὐτά
gen.	αὐτῶν	αὐτῶν	αὐτῶν
dat.	αὐτοῖς	αὐταῖς	αὐτοῖς
acc.	αὐτούς	αὐτάς	αὐτά

11. Conjugation of βλέπω, present active indicative

βλέπω	I see	βλέπομεν	we see
βλέπεις	you (sing.) see	βλέπετε	you (pl.) see
βλέπει	he/she/it sees	βλέπουσι(ν)	they see

12. Conjugation of εἰμί, present active indicative

εἰμί	I am	ἐσμέν	we are
εἶ	you are (sing.)	ἐστέ	you are (pl.)
ἐστί(ν)	he/she/it is	εἰσί(ν)	they are

Index to Greek words _____

Each word is given a short, basic definition, and indexed to the lesson in which it was introduced or studied. Words given only in passing, in examples, are not always included.

word	short definition	lesson
ἀγαθός, ἀγαθή, ἀγαθόν	good, useful	13
ἀγάπη, ἡ	love	4
ἀγαπητός, ἀγαπητή, ἀγαπητόν	beloved	13
ἄγγελος, ὁ	angel, messenger	8
ἅγιος, ἁγία, ἅγιον	sacred, holy	13
Ἀδάμ, ὁ	Adam	13
ἀδελφός, ὁ	brother	3
ἀκούω	I hear	11
ἀλήθεια, ἡ	truth	4
ἀλλά	but, yet	8
ἀναβαίνω	I go up	2
Ἀνδρέας, ὁ	Andrew	10
ἄνθρωπος, ὁ	person, man	3
ἀπό + gen.	from, away from	12
ἀποστέλλω	I send, send out	11
ἀπόστολος, ὁ	apostle	8
Ἄρτεμις, ἡ	Artemis	10
ἀρχή, ἡ	beginning	4
αὐτό	it	15
αὐτός	he, same, --self	11

B

βαπτιστής, ὁ	baptizer	10
Βαρναβᾶς, ὁ	Barnabas	10
βασιλεία, ἡ	kingdom	4
βιβλίον, τό	book	8
βλέπω	I see	2

Γ

γῆ, ἡ	earth, land, soil	14
γραφή, ἡ	writing	4
γράφω	I write	2

Δ

δεσπότης, ὁ	master, owner	10
δηνάριον, τό	denarius	7
διά + acc.	because of	12
διά + gen.	through, during	12
διδάσκω	I teach	2
διδαχή, ἡ	teaching	4
δίκαιος, δικαία, δίκαιον	righteous, just	13
δοῦλος, ὁ	servant/slave	8
δῶρον, τό	gift	7

Ε

ἐγένετο	came into being, was made	15
ἐγώ	I	2
εἰμί	I am	9
εἶπεν	he/she said	11
εἰς + acc.	into	12
ἐκ + gen.	from, out of	12
ἑκατοντάρχης, ὁ	centurion	10
ἐκβάλλω	I drive out, bring forth	13
ἐκκλησία, ἡ	church	4
ἐν + dat.	in	12

ἐντολή, ἡ	commandment	4
ἐξουσία, ἡ	power, authority	4
ἐπαγγελία, ἡ	promise	4
ἐπί + acc.	to, against	12
ἐπί + dat.	at, on the basis of	12
ἐπί + gen.	on, at the time of	12
ἐργάτης, ὁ	worker	10
ἔργον, τό	work, deed	7
ἔσονται	they will be	14
ἔσχατος, ἐσχάτη, ἔσχατον	last, final	13
εὐαγγέλιον, τό	gospel	7
ἔχω	I have	2

Z

ζωή, ἡ	life	4

H

Ἡλίας, ὁ	Elijah, Elias	10
ἡμεῖς	we	2
ἡμέρα, ἡ	day	4
ἡμῶν	our, ours	14
ἦν	he/she/it was	13
Ἡρῴδης, ὁ	Herod	10

Θ

θεός, ὁ	God	3
θησαυρός, ὁ	treasure	3
θρόνος, ὁ	throne	3

I

ἱερόν, τό	temple	7
Ἰησοῦς, ὁ	Jesus	8
ἵππος, ὁ	horse	3

Ἰωάννης, ὁ	John	10

K

καί	and, also	8
καλός, καλή, καλόν	good, honest	13
καρδία, ἡ	heart	4
κατά + acc.	according to, during	12
κατά + gen.	down from, against	12
καταλαμβάνω	I overcome, comprehend	15
κεφαλή, ἡ	head	4
κόσμος, ὁ	world	3
κρίνω	I judge, determine	11
κύριος, ὁ	master, lord	3

Λ

λαμβάνω	I take, I receive	8
λαός, ὁ	the people	11
λέγω	I say	2
λόγος, ὁ	word	3
Λουκᾶς, ὁ	Luke	10

M

μαθητής, ὁ	disciple	10
Μαρία, ἡ	Mary	10
Μᾶρκος, ὁ	Mark	10
μέν	so, then	14
μετά + acc.	after	12
μετά + gen.	with	12
μικρός, μικρά, μικρόν	small	13
μίλιον, τό	Roman mile	7

N

νόμος, ὁ	law	3

Ο

ὁ, ἡ, τό	the	6
οἰκία, ἡ	house	4
ὄνομα, τό	the name	14
οὐρανός, ὁ	heaven	3
οὗτοι	these (people), they	14
οὗτος	this (person), he	15

Π

πάντα	all (things)	15
παρά + acc.	at, alongside	12
παρά + dat.	beside, in the presence of	12
παρά + gen.	from	12
παραβολή, ἡ	parable	4
πᾶς, πᾶσα, πᾶν	all, every	15
Παῦλος, ὁ	Paul	1
περί + acc.	around	12
περί + gen.	about, concerning	12
Πέτρος, ὁ	Peter	1
πίνω	I drink	2
πιστός, πιστή, πιστόν	faithful	13
πονηρός, πονηρά, πονηρόν	wicked, bad	13
ποταμός, ὁ	river	3
πρό + gen.	before	12
πρός + acc.	to	12
προφήτης, ὁ	prophet	10
πρῶτος, πρώτη, πρῶτον	foremost, first	13
πύλη, ἡ	gate	4

Σ

σκοτία, ἡ	the darkness	15
Σολομῶν, ὁ	Solomon	10
στρατιώτης, ὁ	soldier	10

σύ	you (singular)	2
σύν + dat.	with	12

Τ

τέκνον, τό	child	7
τελώνης, ὁ	tax collector	10

Υ

υἱός, ὁ	son	3
ὑπέρ + acc.	over, above	12
ὑπέρ + gen.	on behalf of	12
ὑπηρέτης, ὁ	servant, assistant	10
ὑπό + acc.	under, below	12
ὑπό + gen.	by	12

Φ

φαίνω	I appear, shine	15
φωνή, ἡ	voice	11
φῶς, τό	light	15

Χ

Χριστός, ὁ	Christ	8

Ψ

ψεύστης, ὁ	liar	10

Ω

ὥρα, ἡ	hour	4

* * *

Topic Index _____

Topics are followed by the page, and by the lesson number (e.g., 'L-1') when appropriate.

* * * * * * *

Made in United States
Troutdale, OR
08/02/2023